NOWHERE GIRL
Growing Up Different

My Childhood in a Cult

Nita Clark

ISBN: 1492293377
ISBN 13: 9781492293378
Library of Congress Control Number: 2013916026
CreateSpace Independent Publishing Platform
North Charleston, South Carolina

DEDICATION

This book is dedicated to the children who grew up on The Farm—the ones who came and went, the ones I barely remember, and the ones I'll never forget.

FOREWORD

This is a compelling saga of a very painful past. It should be required reading for all psychotherapists who need to be astute in picking up the clues the clients reveal of the trauma. As a clinical therapist, I have walked beside many courageous clients as they walk this path. I know of the pain they re-experience as they make this journey. Many clients could also benefit from Anita's road map toward healing. It is a difficult but important piece of literature. Thank-you, Anita for your courage.

Donna L. Johnson
L.C.S.W. Retired

AUTHOR'S NOTE

"**A**nita, it sounds like you grew up in a cult," Brian said offhandedly.

This man, probably the fifth counselor to hear my story, spoke his words casually. They threw me off center.

"No. It wasn't a cult!" I shot back. "It was a commune."

As a child, I had no idea what to call our lifestyle. I only knew it was different. In my early thirties, I determined it might have been a commune. Now, here I sat, at forty-seven, in the office of a thirty-something man, still plagued by memories.

"But didn't you have a leader?" he asked. "Didn't everyone follow his commands?"

"Well, yeah ... but it was *not* a cult," I protested. "It was a commune."

Brian glanced at his watch. "Tell you what ... our time is up now," he said, peering at me over his glasses. "From what you've told me, it really sounds like you grew up in a cult. Think about it, that's all I'm saying. We'll discuss it next week. Okay?"

His suggestion was ludicrous. I'd always believed my upbringing was strange ... but a cult? No way! That wasn't possible.

"Sure," I muttered, not intending to give his suggestion another thought. "See you next week."

Driving to my apartment, Brian's words flashed across my mind. *A cult? Is he serious?*

I was living in Clearwater, Florida, my nineteenth move in twenty-seven years ... but who was counting? I was hungry. I stopped at the grocery store for a few dinner items. At the checkout counter, a book about a cult seemed to leap out at me.

While eating, I found myself burning through the pages. Midway into the tenth chapter, my stomach felt queasy. I stopped reading. It was a moment destined to change everything I believed about the first twelve years of my life. It wasn't the actions of the cult followers in the book that rang familiar. It was their mindset ... how they disregarded common sense to follow their leader's commands.

"Oh my God!" I said out loud, "Brian is right! It was a cult."

However, something didn't ring true. Religious dogma had no place in my upbringing. Didn't all cult leaders use religion as a control tactic? Not necessarily, I'd later learn.

From her book, *Cults in Our Midst: The Continuing Fight Against Their Hidden Menace*, Margaret Thaler Singer states: "There is truly a smorgasbord of spiritual, psychological, political and other types of cults and cultic groups seeking adherents and devotees."[1](XXVI)

Our leader—Hal was his name—was a master manipulator, who used psychological means to persuade his followers to conform to his wishes, often to their detriment. Religion had no place in our lives.

For all intents and purposes, Hal was our god. He was all we needed. Religion, he preached, was only a crutch. On sunny days, stormy days, and every day in between, the slogan BECAUSE HAL SAID SO was like an invisible banner, flying high overhead, reminding us that our lives were not our own.

Hal named our property after the Utopian satire, *Erewhon,* written by the nineteenth century novelist, Samuel Butler. But when Hal painted the sign for our

---

1   (Margaret Thaler Singer, *Cults in Our Midst.* Hoboken, NJ: John Wiley & Sons, 2003.

property, he reversed the "w" and "h" so the sign read EREHWON, spelling the word "nowhere" backwards.

Once I finished high school, most of my life was spent running. I imagined that if I traveled far enough, I could leave the residual effects of my childhood behind. Wherever I went, I prayed, "This time will be different. This move will bring relief." It never was, and it never did.

After numerous relocations and job changes (from Washington, D.C. to California, and from the Pentagon to a motion picture studio in Hollywood), a close friend made an interesting observation.

As she watched me pack for yet another venture, she said, "You must be the female version of the Beatle's song, "Nowhere Man." You're always making new plans and moving around so much."

I smiled with her. But inside, I cringed. Of course, she knew nothing about my early days. No one did. That was my secret.

In time, my travels extended to Hawaii, but even paradise couldn't help me to escape the clutches of my past. No matter where I moved, those early memories found my address and managed to color every experience.

After forty-six years of doing the same thing, expecting different outcomes, I finally had had enough. In desperation, I wondered what would happen if instead of running away, I revisited those early years.

To do so required unearthing old memories and then examining the truth behind each one. The book you're about to read is the result of that process.

All of *Nowhere Girl* was written from my personal perspective, as I saw the events, and as they were told to me. Some stories are imaginative re-creations, pieced together from facts, and are not meant to portray events exactly as they occurred. Individual names, and the location where I grew up, have been changed to protect the privacy and dignity of others.

Also, while the name of our property, Erehwon (we pronounced it *Era-whon*), was maintained, it has nothing to do with any other business or farm of that name, now or ever. And even though Hal had officially given our property that fancy handle, all of us simply referred to it as The Farm. Which, I must add, has nothing to do with another well-known commune by that name.

Nowhere Girl is based on my life from ages three to twelve, as I reflect about my feelings and knowledge at that age. If, while reading, you sense you've been left hanging, that's how it was for me, too ... while living through it. Rest assured, everything taking place beyond my awareness will be revealed in the sequence as it was for me.

I'm sure there are as many versions of life on The Farm as there were people who lived through the experience. Some might be more intense than mine, while others much less. Nevertheless, this is my story, told through my eyes.

Nothing herein is intended to be vindictive. Instead, my ultimate hope is that this will be a book of healing ... not just for myself, but for others still harboring secrets from their childhood.

I've heard that we're only as sick as our secrets. Can revealing them finally set us free? That is my prayer.

"Then you will know the truth, and the truth will set you free."
John 8:32 NIV

INTRODUCTION

If you wish to read about a cult where children were schooled within a compound and never saw the outside world, this book may not be for you. My story is about trying to fit in when everything at home is out of sync with the rest of the world.

Although the cult my parents joined was not as complex as those making national headlines, I believe the bond between them and our leader was just as strong. And cults are nothing new. They've been around long before my parents joined their group during the Great Depression.

In writing *Nowhere Girl* I hope to bring awareness to the smaller cults within our society, as well as draw attention to the fact that many cults are not religion based. My purpose is to shine a light on the fate facing children growing up in a cult setting.

Margaret Thaler Singer was a clinical psychologist and bestselling author. In the 1960's she began studying the nature of cults and mind control. Since she is somewhat of an expert on the subject, here are some quotes from her book, *Cults in Our Midst*, regarding frequently asked questions about cults. All quotes from *Cults in Our Midst* are reproduced in this book with permission of John Wiley & Sons, Inc.

What is a cult, and how does the leader wield his power?

"A cult is a mirror of what is inside the cult leader. He has no restraints on him. He can make his fantasies and desires come alive in the world he creates around him. He can lead people to do his bidding. He can make the surrounding world really his world. What most cult leaders achieve is akin to the fantasies of a child at play, creating a world with toys and utensils. In that play world, the child feels omnipotent and creates a realm of his own for a few minutes or a few hours. He moves the toy dolls about. They do his bidding. They speak his words back to him. He punishes them any way he wants. He is all-powerful and makes his fantasy come alive." (254)

"The cult leader's idiosyncratic notions permeate the system he puts into operation. There is no feedback. No criticism is allowed. When he finally gets his followers to be sufficiently obedient, he can wield unlimited power and get his followers to carry out whatever acts he directs. He becomes the most powerful director one can imagine." (255)

What about the role of parents?

"In cults, parents do not function as they do in the regular world. They are more like middle-management personnel in a business: the cult leader dictates how children are to be reared, and the parents simply implement those orders. (245)

"Parents in cults are like offspring of the leader and are expected to be his obedient children." (254)

What is it like for the children?

"Cult children do not see adults having input in decision making or making ideas and plans together. Instead, they witness and are taught that critical, evaluative thinking, new ideas, and independent ideas get people in trouble. From this, they learn simply to obey." (258)

"Cult children are powerless. They are total victims—even the parents on whom they should be able to depend are controlled by the cult leader, and thus the children's fate is in his hands." (245)

Who joins a cult?

"Despite the myth that normal people don't get sucked into cults, it has become clear over the years that everyone is susceptible to the lure of these master manipulators. In fact, the majority of adolescents and adults in cults come from middle-class backgrounds, are fairly well educated, and are not seriously disturbed prior to joining." (17)

Why don't cult followers leave?

"There is no simple answer to that question, for a variety of factors contribute to keeping a cult member bound to the group. In most cases, there is no physical restraint, although some groups do punish and imprison those who try to leave. But in all cases, there is a psychological bond that becomes most difficult to sever." (266)

"The final factor that closes the trap's door is the cult member's active participation. Whether or not you care to admit it, you have invested in cult life. It's hard to leave that—partly because there is still part of you that wants to believe this really is going to work, and partly because of the shame and the guilt you feel." (273)

Author's comment: My experience was completely different from the children born into the cult in Waco, Texas. However, after seeing a newspaper photo of one of those young girls, I felt a strong connection to her. The picture was snapped as she left the compound before the fire. She was in a car getting ready to be driven to safety. In her blank stare, I saw myself.

EREHWON FAMILY TREE

When I was three, the Erehwon Family Tree looked like this:

LEADER'S FAMILY	CHILDREN	AGE
HAL AND EDITH	ELIZABETH	10
	CARTER	8
	DARLA	2

HAL'S BROTHER'S FAMILY		
CHARLIE AND SONYA	DENNIS	8
	JULIE	6
	GREG	5
	JOEY	1

MY PARENTS		
NICK AND ELLIE	GINA	9
	KERRI	7
	TODD	5
	NITA	3

OTHER GROWN-UPS

TED AND DEBBIE	BOBBY	9
	JANET	7
BILL AND TERESA	JOHNNY	5

Plus two or three other couples and their children

PROLOGUE

1951

It's the summer before my third school year. I'm lying on my parents' bed. Although I'm in a house full of children and grown-ups, I feel completely alone. That's nothing new. I spend a great deal of time by myself—lost in my own world of make-believe. That's how I cope with the lifestyle I've grown to hate.

Sounds of playful banter filter up the stairs. I wonder what game the other kids are playing. Monopoly? Clue? Canasta?

The sun streaming across the foot of the bed invites me over to the window. I see the older kids on the baseball field. It's Todd's turn at bat. My brother is nine and a half—only two years older than me. Normally, I like watching him play baseball, but on this day I don't care if he gets a hit or not. I have more important things in mind.

I walk over to the doorway and peer into the hall. I want to make sure no one is coming. It's a large, square space, with three bedrooms and a bathroom branching off. Sometimes we play jacks or card games here.

Other times we pull two doors together to create an elevator. There's a hole in the wall (that no one has bothered to fix) from the doorknobs hitting too hard, or too many times.

Across from my parents' bedroom is a room where all the girls sleep. I share a bottom bunk with our leader's youngest daughter. To the left is our bathroom, and to the right our leader and his wife sleep some of the time. Nothing is very certain on The Farm. That includes lots of things ... like sleeping arrangements and when I'll see Mom and Dad again.

I sure miss my parents. Once they were home all day, working long, hard hours, from milking cows to bailing hay. However, about the time I turned five, all of that changed. They started working in the city, about a million miles away. Actually, I have no idea how far they travel each day. They leave before I wake up, and return after I'm asleep.

The farmwomen take turns caring for the children. None of them are like a mom to me. I don't know from one day to the next who will be watching me, if anyone. Most days I'm left on my own, with no one seeming to care what I do, or where I go. Oh sure, I have enough food—that isn't a problem. But still, I'm starving to death for someone to hold me and tell me I'm special.

Sunday is my favorite day of the week. That's when Mom and Dad are home all day. Saturdays are my second favorite. Mom begins work later that day. While she "paints her face," I get to hear her sing rousing renditions of songs from the movies.

Sometimes Mom is a lot of fun. Other times, she gets mad really fast. Then BAM! Everything changes. Like the time my sister, Gina, had a plate broken over her head to instill some sort of wisdom. Or when Mom threatened to push my sister, Kerri, under a huge semi truck to teach her to stay away from the road in front of our house.

Truth is, most of Mom's lessons don't get taken seriously. Like training Todd to wait his turn to use the bathroom. His warm pee, squirting in my lap (as I sat on the pot), proved that lecture had been ignored.

As for me ... I have a scar on the back of my hand. It's an iron burn, reminding me not to play near the ironing board.

Even so, there are times Mom teaches us fun things, like tap dancing to "School Days," mastering the Charleston, and how to Shuffle off to Buffalo.

Now that Mom has a job in the city, she dresses a lot fancier than the other farmwomen. They usually wear tattered housedresses. Mom is a lot prettier, too—with deep dimples, long brown hair, and the most beautiful smile in the whole world.

Personally, I think Mom is a lot happier since she's been working away from home. To make up for how much I miss her, I spend a lot of time in her room. That's where I found an escape route into a world where everyone adores me, and wants to be with me.

By placing rocks in the tips of my shoes, I'm transformed into a beautiful ballerina, twirling in front of Mom's full-length mirror. Sure, I fall down a lot, but what are a few spills and tumbles compared with the adoration from my make-believe crowd?

Other times, a bath towel, draped into a mink stole, turns me into a glamorous movie star. I call these secret escapades "talking to the wall." Being a bit embarrassed about all this, I try hard to quit. But a strange force keeps pulling me back.

This morning began like any other. Nothing bad has happened. But something *is* about to happen. I can feel it in every part of my body.

I walk over to my father's tall chest of drawers and pull out the middle compartment (the one designated as mine), and start rummaging through it.

I want to tell someone I need more space, but I'm sure no one will listen. There is a tiny closet in the corner of the Girls' Room. It's reserved for our leader's oldest daughter. I share a metal rack with the other girls.

A quick check through my drawer reveals nothing very useful for the task at hand. As I move toward my mother's dresser, I almost hear her boasting that she has the prettiest one on The Farm. Searching through her top drawer, my hand momentarily rests on a small wooden chest where she keeps important papers like birth certificates and such.

I remember her telling my two older sisters, Todd and me, "If there's ever a fire, grab that box."

Rarely do I ever peek inside. I did once ... about a year ago. That's when I wrote a brief note to Mom and tucked it safely inside. I figured she'd find it eventually, and surely if she knew ...

However, thanks to my brother, Mom never saw that note. Shortly after writing it, I caught him snickering.

"Did you really write this?" he teased, his finger pointing inches from my face.

"Of course not," I lied, snatching it from his hand and crumpling my feelings into oblivion.

Why did I even bother? No one cares how I feel anyway.

Now, I'm a whole year older. Now I have something different in mind.

I continue my search. Make-up? Nope. Comb? No. Nail file? Yep, that should do it.

Mom's dresser is flush against the wall. It's heavy. I struggle to pull it out and at an angle.

Okay! That'll do.

I stab the file tip into the hard surface, frantically scraping it back and forth. Touching the file's edge, I grin. Good! Still sharp.

I scratch away for what feels like hours. Finally finished, I step back and look at my name, N-I-T-A, in big block letters. Perfect!

No doubt my mother will scream at me when she sees my handiwork. But for the moment, I couldn't care less. I walk downstairs and climb onto the living room couch with the tattered coverlet haphazardly tossed about. I remember the note I'd scribbled to Mom the year before. Three words in block letters had said it all: I HATE MYSELF.

I gaze out the window. Several kids are playing kick the can in the front yard. I'm not in the mood for games. Soon, the smell of fried chicken drifting from the kitchen warns me that I don't have much time. I need to escape.

Collapsing into the couch cushions, I bring my knees into a fetal position. Before drifting off, I pray with all my might to a God I know nothing about. "Please, God. When I wake up let me be in a normal family. I want to be normal. Please, God. Please."

Normal ... normal ... I lull myself to sleep.

PART ONE

A CULT IS BORN

How does a group of intelligent young adults turn their will and mind over to another? Every story has a back-story. Mine is no exception.

My parents joined their group during the Great Depression, a time when many workers were unemployed. Businesses were failing, and people were jumping from skyscrapers in New York City. With such a devastating backdrop, their guru's ideas must have sounded exciting, his dream promising, and his plans hopeful.

While many details died with the cult members, much of what took place was captured through stories collected over decades. The stories presented here are not meant to portray events exactly as they occurred, but rather to suggest the essence, to the best of my knowledge, about what transpired.

It all began many years before The Farm ...

CHAPTER 1

1920

"I don't understand, Melvin. Why can't you get a job around here like everyone else? There's got to be some kind of work in Cleveland! That job you're taking in the country can't pay much. What does it pay? It can't be much."

As the argument continued, their youngest son, Charlie, huddled in the corner of an upstairs bedroom. He turned to his older brother. He was reading a book on the top bunk.

"What are they fighting about now?" Charlie asked. "And why do they have to scream so loud?"

Hal shook his head. "That's the way they are. Turn up the radio. That's what I do."

Their mother didn't seem to like her husband even a little bit. She never really loved him. Their marriage had been arranged, and over the years, Melvin had become increasingly more difficult. Most of the time he was just plain mean. In fact, behind his back, people would say things like, "Did you hear what Mean Melvin did now?"

No one ever said such things to his face. They wouldn't dare. Melvin was a man to fear.

"Why do you have to work so far away?" his wife asked. You know how difficult the kids can be."

"Damn it! You know there aren't any jobs around here. Anyway, I told you, this is only temporary ... just till we get back on our feet." Melvin glanced around. "Where are the kids? Where's Hal? I need to talk to him." Not giving his wife a chance to answer, he walked over to the living room stairway and yelled, "Harold! Get down here!"

"Don't worry, Charlie," Hal said, putting his arm around his nine-year-old brother. "Someday I'll get us out of here. But right now, I've got to talk to Dad. Be right back. I promise."

The two boys walked to the top of the stairway. Charlie watched his brother descend the stairs; then returned to the closet.

When Hal reached the dining room, he found his father sitting at the head of the table, as if waiting to carve a Thanksgiving turkey.

"Hi, Dad. Did you want me?"

"About time you got down here. Where's your little brother?"

"Doing his homework, I guess."

"Yeah-yeah-yeah. Come here and sit down."

Hal did as instructed.

"I have something to tell you, but first maybe you can tell *me* something. What the hell is going on with your grades? Your mother tells me you're practically flunking that psychology class. Think you're such a big shot, don't ya? Gonna be a famous psychiatrist some day, right?" His voice had a mocking tone. "Yeah, well, I know better. You know better, too ... don't ya, Hal?" His father didn't wait for an answer. "You know, maybe if you'd study more."

"I study plenty. And I'm not failing anything!"

"Really? I doubt it. You can't do anything right. Never could."

"Yes, I can. I love college. Especially psychology."

"Don't talk back to me," he said, raising his hand, poised to strike.

Closing his eyes, Hal braced for the blow.

"And don't start crying, you big baby. You had that coming. Geez ... can't you do anything right? You're never gonna amount to anything. And you know what I'm talking about, don't-cha, Fatso?"

At nineteen, Hal was only slightly chubby. Still, his father seemed to relish in calling him Fatso. "Your one big, fat nothin', you know that? Yeah, you know it. So why don't you give up already?" Disgust filled Melvin's face. "You're nothing. A zero! That's all you'll ever be!" he screamed before walking away.

When his father left the room, Hal took off for the stairway.

He'd taken two steps when his father called after him. "Hold it right there, Harold," he said. "I'm not done talking. Do you think you can keep that big trap of yours shut while I tell you something? Can you do that for me, you little baby? And damn it, look at me when I talk to you!"

Hal didn't move. His legs were stiff, eyes forward—like a soldier standing at attention.

"I-I-I'm sorry, Dad."

"You're sorry, *who*? Damn it, Hal ... you know better."

"I'm sorry, *sir.*"

His father nodded. "That's more like it."

Hal remained motionless.

"Listen Hal, I got a job in the country ... about fifty miles from here. You know how long I've been out of work. Well, guess what? There ain't no work around here. Not a damn thing."

Hal didn't move.

"I'll be working on a farm. It's hard work," his father went on. "But it's all I could find. I'll be living there most of the time, but don't be getting any stupid ideas. Your mother will let me know if you give her any trouble. And I expect you to take care of Charlie, too. Do you understand me, Hal? Well, do you?"

"Yes, sir. I understand, sir."

"Good! Okay, that's all. You can go now."

Hal mounted the stairs two at a time.

He slid beside his brother in the closet. "Did ya hear that, Charlie? Did ya hear that? Dad is leaving. Isn't that great news?" Hal sounded as excited as a six-year-old on Christmas morning. "I'm sure he'll be coming home sometimes, but there won't be any more Mean Melvin bossing us around. Isn't that great, Charlie?"

Charlie smiled, said nothing; then he rested his head on Hal's shoulder.

CHAPTER 2

1923

By 1923, Hal was a stocky twenty-two-year-old. He had a captivating smile and dark, slicked-back hair. Although he wasn't very attractive, any shortcomings in the "looks" department were nicely overshadowed by his charm and charisma.

Hal and his family were struggling financially. His father's job in the country didn't provide much income and none of it went to his children.

With little monetary wherewithal, Hal feared he might have to drop out of college.

One morning, feeling somewhat unsure of his future, Hal telephoned Donna. Romance wasn't the bond between them. Instead, he viewed Donna as a true friend, one who could see the brighter side of any situation. He decided that meeting her for coffee was exactly what he needed.

Hal walked to the corner drugstore in the rain; then selected a counter stool near the window. When Donna arrived, he greeted her enthusiastically. But soon his smile faded. "Hey, what's wrong?" he asked, guiding her to the stool beside him. "You don't look so good."

"Oh, Hal ... It's Joanne. You remember her, right? The girl you thought was so much fun last weekend?"

"Oh, yeah. Great gal. What's wrong? Did something happen?"

A waitress in a pale blue uniform walked over. "What can I get you two," she asked cheerfully.

Hal waved a hand. "Just coffee, thanks."

When she left, Donna cried. "Oh, Hal, It's horrible. It's just horrible."

"Tell me," he said, pleading. "What is it? Is Joanne okay?"

"No! No, she's not okay. She'll never be okay, Hal," she said, sobbing. "Joanne committed suicide last night."

"What? No! Oh my God! Why?"

"I don't know," she said. "It's impossible to understand."

They sipped their coffee in silence.

Hal pushed his cup away. "It's gonna be okay," he said, his voice filled with compassion. He stared out at the rain, his arm around her shoulders. "It's gonna be okay," he said again.

Donna jerked his arm away. When she spoke, her words had an angry edge. "No! It *won't* be okay, Hal. Joanne's gone." More tears came.

Hal pulled a handkerchief from his shirt pocket and tenderly wiped away her tears. "I'm so sorry, Donna," he said. "I'm so sorry."

The two sat in silence. Then Hal spoke the words he'd been mulling over. "Donna," he said softly, "Joanne must have felt trapped."

Donna glanced up. "Oh Hal, how do you know that?"

"I just know. That's all. I just know." He looked out the window, as if deep in thought. "Joanne *must* have felt trapped," he said. "Otherwise, she wouldn't have killed herself. I only wish I could have done something," he added, barely above a whisper.

And then, somewhere between repeating how sorry he was and telling her that everything would be okay, his voice became enthusiastic.

"Donna," he said. "I just realized what I want to do with my life. I'm gonna be a psychiatrist," he said confidently. "Sure, I took a few courses in college. They were interesting and all that. But now, after hearing about Joanne, I—"

"But Hal, you told me you don't have tuition money. You can't be a psychiatrist without a degree. And besides, I talked with Joanne's mother. Joanne was depressed ... had been for years." She turned away. "Face it Hal, we can't prevent the inevitable."

Hal shook his head. "No! I disagree. I don't believe that. This wouldn't have happened if someone had given her some guidance."

He gazed into Donna's eyes. "Why do you suppose Joanne felt trapped? Do you think it was her studies? Or maybe—"

"Oh, Hal," Donna interrupted. "We don't know what went wrong."

"That's my point," he said. "We *should* have known." He paused. "Don't you see, Donna? Joanne needed support."

For a long while, they sat without talking.

"I only wish I could have done something, that's all," Hal said finally.

Donna turned to face him. "Oh Hal," she said. "You'd make a great psychiatrist."

"Donna, I don't know how I'm gonna do it. I certainly don't know where I'll get the money. But there's one thing I know for sure. I'm gonna help people like Joanne. I'm gonna get that degree. Nothing is gonna stop me."

However, when next semester's tuition money was due, Hal simply didn't have the funds. He had to drop out of college.

CHAPTER 3

1931

At thirty, Hal was struggling financially. He'd remained close friends with Donna. At the start of each week, the two of them would meet for coffee and conversation.

"How's everything going?" Donna asked one Monday morning, slipping next to him in her usual spot.

"Not so good."

"I know. Not much better here. I can't find a job anywhere. Too bad you couldn't finish college. Thanks to this damn depression, I'm sure lots of people *need* psychiatrists."

"Yeah, well, it wasn't possible." Hal leaned over and picked up a newspaper lying on the counter. The two sat in silence while Hal scanned articles. Then he tapped his finger on a front-page headline. "Check this out, will ya?" he said. "Unemployment climbs to 16.3 percent." He pulled that page out and handed it to Donna. "When's this country gonna get out of the mess we're in?" he said. Then he thumbed through sections until he located the sports page. "Ah, that's better."

The two friends sipped coffee while reading.

All at once, Donna sat up straight and gazed into Hal's eyes. "Hold on!" she said. "You can still help people. For God's sake, Hal, nobody can find work. Everyone's losing hope." She gawked at him. "Hal, don't ya see. These people *need* you."

His face turned angry. "Donna, I *told* you. I don't have money for a degree."

"I know that," she said, but maybe you don't *need* a degree. Listen," she said, pointing to another horrific headline, "do you honestly think these people are gonna care if you have a degree or not?"

"Well, I—"

"Wait! I know what you can do," Donna interjected. "You can hold group meetings in your living room. Your mom probably wouldn't mind. And your father is rarely home, anyway. Right?"

"Well, yeah. But—"

"You can even charge a little something for each session.

"I don't know. I—"

"Oh, Hal," Donna said. "If anyone can do it, you can.

All conversation stopped while Hal signaled the waitress for a coffee refill.

"Y'know, Donna," he said, watching as the dark liquid was poured into his cup. "I think you just might have something here."

"I know," she said smiling. "I think I just might."

***

Within a month, Hal, Donna, and several friends were meeting around the kitchen table in Hal's home. As the weeks advanced, so did the number of participants. In two months, the gatherings expanded into his living room.

An avid reader, Hal introduced his favorite authors to his eager students. He proclaimed one of Alfred Adler's books to be their bible. He discussed and analyzed books by James Branch Cabell and Samuel Butler, giving his own interpretations about the authors' writings. His lectures, delivered during one of the worst economic slumps in U.S. history, focused on happiness, hope, and promise.

In time, Hal grew instinctively aware of which words and phrases would captivate his audience. During each session, hope and encouragement were offered to his students. In return, they lavished adoration and loyalty upon him. This give and take process was perfected over time. The more support he offered, the more power he took.

Not to say it didn't work both ways. The more admiration his students bestowed upon him, the more hope they received. So it was a win-win situation for all.

Six months later, Donna got married and moved out of town. However, the seed of her idea had not only blossomed. It was thriving.

CHAPTER 4

1932

At twenty-one, Charlie was an attractive man with light brown, wavy hair. He had a cleft chin, and his smile was endearing. He was in excellent shape, stood about six feet tall, and had an easy-going nature. Hal, ten years older, had a receding hairline and was considered short. His tendency toward being overweight had become more pronounced, and fits of anger had started to interfere with his usual charming persona.

The brothers' interests were also quite different. Hal spent most of his time reading and preparing weekly lectures. Charlie toured the Great Lakes area with a jazz band.

Although Charlie was usually busy playing his trumpet, Hal never stopped hoping he would attend one of his study groups. One day, he was pleasantly surprised when Charlie responded favorably to his invitation.

"Tell ya what," Charlie said, carefully placing his trumpet in its case, "How 'bout if I join you next Sunday? I'll have the weekend off," he said, winking at his brother. "By the way, how many are in your group now?"

"Well, let's see ... not counting me and Edith, there's Frank, Gloria, Lou, Barbara, Rudy, Ruth, and Ellie. They're my regulars. Nick comes occasionally, but I never know for sure about him. He's such a lady's man ... doesn't always have time for us."

Hal and Charlie chuckled.

"So, let's see," Hal continued, "if you show up, and Nick decides to grace us with his presence, I guess that'll make eleven." He paused. "Hey, why don't you bring that girl you've been seeing? Sonya, isn't it?"

"Yep, she's terrific. And I'll tell ya, that girl sure can dance. Went all the way to New York City by herself trying to make it on Broadway. She'd have made it too, if her brother hadn't gone after her."

Hal grinned. "I'd love to meet her. Sounds like a real live wire."

"She is. See for yourself ... I'll bring her next Sunday."

"Great! The two of you will make it an even dozen." Then he added, "Oh, I almost forgot ... Barbara is bringing a friend tonight." He grabbed another chair from the kitchen and added it to the others.

Charlie walked to the front door with his trumpet. He was a popular member of the band and rarely got nervous on stage. In fact, Charlie never seemed bothered about anything.

"See ya later," Charlie called over his shoulder. "Some of us need to earn a living."

They both laughed. "Tell Mom I'll grab a bagel and lox later," Charlie said as he slipped out the front door.

Supper for Hal was oxtail soup with his mother. It certainly wasn't his favorite meal. Nor was it his mother's. She would much rather fix a proper Jewish meal of schnitzel and kugel. However, considering the state of the economy, such family favorites were not an option. While Hal helped his mother tidy up the kitchen, he persuaded her to visit the woman next door.

"Be neighborly," Hal told her. But, really he wanted the house to himself.

Edith was the first to arrive for the study group. Hal had been seeing this no frills, nineteen-year-old, for several months. She loved attending her boyfriend's meetings, and often wore a navy blue dress for the occasion.

Other times, she chose a gray skirt and white cotton blouse. Tonight it was the classic navy.

Hal greeted her with a quick hello. "Time to get the coffee brewing," he said after Edith hung up her coat. "Hey ... and put the kettle on for tea, will ya?" he added, taking a stack of notes to the table.

Edith was twelve years younger than Hal. Prior to meeting him, she had been ill at ease around anyone of the opposite sex, let alone one so much older.

"Sure. Be glad to. I can see you've got things to do." She gazed at him with adoring eyes. "You sit tight," she said before scurrying into the kitchen to get started.

The longer her relationship with Hal progressed, the more Edith's subservient side became pronounced. She never questioned Hal or talked back. And if she was jealous when he flirted with the other girls, she never said a word. Besides, wasn't he supposed to make everyone feel comfortable? Didn't he need to make them feel loved?

Edith was placing cups around the table as the first guest arrived. Barbara knocked three times and then walked in. Even at twenty, she had a mature, heavyset appearance. Still, she had a warm smile, and her affection for Hal was obvious. A rather thin girl followed close behind. Her stylish, light brown hair, looked like she had just returned from the beauty shop. Her dress was simple, yet fashionable. The two of them made quite a pair of opposites. Barbara's jacket was shabby while her friend's full-length coat had the sophistication of Saks Fifth Avenue.

"Hello Barbara," Edith called out. "Good to see you." She hurried across the room. "And who is this?" she asked, smiling at Barbara's guest.

Barbara wasn't in the mood for Edith's small talk. It was Hal she came to see. She grabbed her friend's hand, and led her past Edith.

"Hi there," she said, while approaching the man she admired most in the world. "Told you I'd bring someone tonight," she said almost singing the words. "I'm glad Jake didn't mind picking her up."

"Tell me," Hal said sarcastically. "How's your husband doing these days?"

Barbara rolled her eyes. "Oh, he's his usual boring self." Then in her "good little girl" voice she added, "This is the gal I told you about." Her hands went on the shoulders of Hal's potential new student. "Hal, this is Deborah." She raised an eyebrow. "Deborah hails from Shaker Heights. Her father is a doctor, doncha know. A surgeon no less."

Hal took an extra half step forward, putting himself almost uncomfortably close to Deborah. He extended his hand. She took it.

"Well … hello there, Deborah," he said, his hand lingering a little too long after the handshake. "So glad you could join us tonight." Then, noticing others arriving, Hal excused himself. "Be right back," he said.

As Hal chatted with other guests, he occasionally glanced over at Deborah.

From across the room, Edith was watching. She walked over to her boyfriend. "Hal … wasn't it nice of Barbara to bring a friend?" she asked.

Ignoring her comment, Hal returned to Deborah's side.

Edith joined them and tried again. "Hal, wasn't it nice of Barbara to bring someone tonight?"

Hal's next words sounded dream-like. His gaze held Deborah's. "Yeah, nice," he said; then added, "Tell me, what brings you here tonight, Deborah?"

"Well," she said. "I've certainly heard great things about you."

"Oh, I don't know about that," he said.

"Yeah, well Barbara tells me you're pretty amazing."

Hal placed a hand on Barbara's shoulder. "Well … I think our good friend might be a little bit biased," he said with a chuckle.

"You're probably right," Deborah said. "I know she sure loves attending your lectures."

"So glad Barbara brought you," he said, his eyes studying Deborah.

Deborah smiled. "And what's this about an island?" she asked. "I hear you're planning to find an island in the Pacific where you and your students can live." She cocked her head. "Is that true?"

Hal snickered. "Let me guess. Barbara told you, right?"

"Sure did," Barbara, said, looking pleased to be back in the conversation.

"Okay, I confess," he said, laughing. "Guilty as charged. I promise I'll tell you all about it later, my dear."

Hal sauntered over to the table and gallantly pulled out a chair.

"For you, Deborah." He grinned boyishly. "I want you next to me tonight."

Deborah sat. Barbara selected the chair beside her.

"Sorry, ladies, Hal said. "As much as I'd love to schmoose with you two, I'd better go mingle."

With Hal out of earshot, Barbara nudged Deborah. "Told you he was amazing," she said, winking.

Edith had been listening. She patted her thin hair, and tucked her dark curls in place. She sighed; then sat down in her usual place near the kitchen.

Hal glanced around. "Grab a chair," he said, heading to the table. "Let's begin."

He waited until the others were seated, and then said, "Before I do anything else, I want to thank Barbara for bringing a friend tonight." He gave her a wink. "All of you should be as loyal and faithful as Barbara."

He turned to his guest of honor. "And this lovely lady on my right is Deborah." He made a grand, sweeping gesture with his arm. "Deborah, he said, "This is everyone."

The room started buzzing with friendly conversation.

Hal called his meeting to order. Then he turned over his notes. "I have a new topic tonight," he said. "But first, I promised Deborah I'd share information about our island." He hesitated slightly. "Well, I don't have a specific island in mind, but I have set up my first rule. And it's an important one." He paused, making sure he had everyone's full attention. "Only married couples can move to the island. That's my number one rule." He smiled. "No single folks allowed."

"Why?" Barbara asked. "I don't mean to interrupt, but why does everyone need to be married?"

"Simple," he said. "The whole idea is to form our own community. Your children will marry your children," he said pointing on one side of the room. "And your children will marry your children," he added, gesturing toward the others.

"I get it," Barbara said, beaming. "We'll be one big, happy family."

"Yep," Hal said. "That's the idea. But I have another subject to discuss." He raised his voice. "Relationships ... love for one another. That's our topic tonight. It's people that matter most."

His eyes scanned the room. "Without people, what do you have?" His voice got louder. "Nothing!" he said, staring at them. "And what about money? Can money buy you happiness? Ever?" He grinned. "No. Money can't buy what you really need. Sure, it's true. None of us have much since the Depression hit. But we have something money can't buy. Isn't that right Ellie?"

Ellie jumped. "W-what?" she said, startled. Ellie had been sitting in the corner, diligently taking notes. She searched through her papers. "Well ... yes, I —"

Hal cut her off. "Ellie," he said, "don't think about what you *should* say. Forget all about your notes. You've made a lot of new friends here, right?"

"Oh, yes!" she added enthusiastically. "Yes, I sure have."

"Then why don't you stand up and tell us how important relationships are?"

Ellie slowly stood. When she spoke, her smile showed off her dimples. "I'm happier than I've ever been," she said. "I love these people."

"Thanks Ellie. You can sit down now. You said it very well. We all need each other. Nothing in the world is more important."

Hal spoke for quite a long while, occasionally calling on others for their input. When his lecture ended, he walked into the kitchen.

Returning with a fresh cup of coffee, he placed it in front of Deborah.

"Oh! Thank you," Deborah said, accepting his kindness.

"I loved having you here tonight," he said warmly. Then his voice took on a begging quality. "Please come back again," he said. "I need you here."

Deborah offered a shy smile. "I'll try."

He stroked her arm. "You'll try? Is that the best you can do? I need to see you again, Deborah. I need you here."

"Oh! I don't know," she said. "You look like you hold the world in the palm of your hand."

"Hardly," Hal said. "But maybe ... maybe if I saw more of you I would." Then he let out an embarrassed laugh, "Oh, will ya listen to me go on and on. What I'm trying to say, and doing a rather poor job of it, is ... I'd like you to come back next week. That's all I'm saying. Will you, please?"

Barbara was there, holding out Deborah's coat. "We gotta go," she said, peeking through the window curtains. "Jake's a real bear if he has to wait."

Deborah slipped on her coat. She made a waving gesture. "Bye, everyone," she said. "It was nice meeting all of you."

Hal accompanied both girls to the door.

Before she stepped outside, Deborah smiled at Hal. "Oh, and Hal," she said, "call me Debbie, okay?"

"Sure!" Hal said, chuckling as he called after her. "See ya next week, Debbie."

Hal mingled with the other group members, but his mind wasn't with them. He excused himself, went to the kitchen, and turned the knob under the kettle.

He squeezed a lemon wedge together, letting the juice drip into his cup of Lipton's. He sat at the kitchen table, slumped back in his chair, and stretched out his legs. Slowly, he sipped his tea.

"Yeah, Debbie's a nice girl all right," he said under his breath. "But what that girl can do for me might be a whole lot nicer."

CHAPTER 5

NOVEMBER 1935 TO MARCH 1939

On the third Sunday in November 1935, Nick took a bus over to pick up Ellie. He had escorted her home from Hal's study group the week before. Together, they rode another bus to Hal's house. They arrived as Debbie's car was pulling into the driveway. She had been attending Hal's study group every week without fail.

Debbie swung open the door of her Lincoln. "Come on," she said. "We don't want to miss anything."

Hal's session began with a cordial greeting, but halfway through his lecture, he violently threw his papers across the room. "You guys make me sick," he said. "You say you believe in me. You act like you're listening, but you don't do anything I tell you. You're nothing but a bunch of hypocrites! Can't you do one thing I ask? I've told you a million times ... only married couples can live on the island? So, when are you guys gonna get married already?" He took a breath. "Okay, fine! Tell you what. Next week Edith and I will go to New York. I know a place where they don't make ya wait around for blood tests. Any of you guys care to join us?"

It took a while for Edith to recover from the shock of her boyfriend's announcement. It was the first time she'd heard anything about getting married. However, soon enough she began acting like they'd been planning their big day for months.

Before the week ended, Hal made good on his promise. Charlie and Sonya joined them in New York, exchanging vows on the same day. So did Frank and Gloria, Lou and Ruth, and another couple who had just joined the study group.

A month and a half later, Ellie was talking to several of the newlyweds before Hal's meeting.

"What are you so excited about, Ellie?" Hal asked. "Besides, where's your ring? Why haven't you and Nick tied the knot yet?" he asked with a cynical smile.

Her eyes went down.

"Ellie, look at me when I talk to you," he said. "I asked you a simple question. Answer me!" he bellowed.

Tears started to flow. "Hal, what do you want me to say?" she pleaded.

"I don't want you to say anything," he said with a sarcastic edge. "There's nothing you *can* say, is there? That's because you didn't listen to me. What did I tell you to do last month? What did I tell you, Ellie?"

Ellie was too upset to try to understand what Hal expected her to say. She covered her face in her hands and started to sob.

"Look at you," he said. "Can't you do anything except sit there crying like a baby? Listen, little girl, I can't do everything for you. You have to do *some* things for yourself." He paused. "Oh, forget it," he said. "You never listen to anything I say. And quit hiding your face!"

Ellie reluctantly withdrew her hands. "I think—"

"Damn it, Ellie. You don't *need* to think. Just do what I tell you!"

The tension in the room escalated.

"You did hear me tell everyone to get married, didn't you?" He paused momentarily. "Well, didn't you?" He glared at her with contempt. "Ya know what," he said, shaking his head dismissively, "forget it Ellie."

His attention turned to Nick. "What's the matter, Nick? Why haven't you married Ellie yet?" Nick started to speak, but Hal cut him off. "Oh, yeah. That's right.

You're a lady's man, going by the name Jack Gold ... so you can chase those nice Jewish girls at the clubs. Isn't that right, Mr. Gold?"

Hal turned back to Ellie. "He's never gonna marry you, ya know. He's too much in love with the single life. He doesn't want you. And he must not want to live on the island either," he said, his voice oozing with sarcasm. "Tell ya what, why don't the two of you just sit there and keep your big traps shut!"

"But Hal," Nick protested. "I—"

"Save it Nick. I don't want to hear it."

Finally, Hal addressed the others. "Now ... where was I?" he said, as if glad to be back on topic.

When Hal noticed Nick and Ellie cowering in the corner, his anger fired up again. "That's it!" he said. "Nick ... Ellie ... Get out! Get the hell out of my house!"

They didn't move.

"Don't you get it?" Hal said. "I'm finished with you two. Some people in this room *do* know how to listen to me." He nodded to the couples that had gotten married with him. "So, even though the two of you would love to sit there like little mice in the corner, I don't want you here."

His full attention went to Nick. "Well! Don't just sit there like a dead fish, Nick. Go get your coats. Get out!"

Nick jumped up, pulled their coats off the rack in the hallway, and practically shoved Ellie out the front door.

Once outside, they picked up speed. When they reached the corner, Ellie burst into tears. Nick put his arm around her, but Ellie was beyond consoling.

"What happened in there?" Ellie said. "That didn't even sound like Hal." Nick pulled out his handkerchief and offered it to her. "How can Hal expect us to get married? I haven't known you very long."

"I know, I know," Nick said, dabbing at her tears. "But ya know, Ellie," he began slowly, "we'll probably be getting married sooner or later. Right?"

"I ... I guess so."

"Well, it might as well be sooner," he said, smiling.

It was midweek before Ellie called Nick with her answer. "I thought it over and you're right," she said. "We can drive to New York, get married, and be back by Sunday."

And that's what they did, without any friends or family members present.

Nick and Ellie attended Hal's next study group as husband and wife. Feeling a bit uneasy about being there, they positioned themselves in the back of the room. When Hal became aware of their presence, his tone changed from pleasant to furious. "What are you two doing here?" he said, his voice escalating.

Nick offered a weak smile. "We got married," he said, timidly. "Last Friday."

"Well now, isn't that nice to hear?" Hal said, his whole demeanor softening. He hurried to the table and pulled out two chairs. "Sit down, sit down," he said. "There's a lot you two can learn tonight."

After his lecture ended, Hal approached the newlyweds. "You don't mind if I borrow your wife, do you, Nick?" he said, whisking Ellie away.

In the kitchen, Hal pulled Ellie into a warm embrace. When he released his hold, he stared deeply into her eyes. "Oh, Ellie," he said after a moment. "You know I love you, don't you?"

"Y-yes," she stammered.

"You'd better," he said. "I never wanted to get mad at you. Honest. But, Ellie, you gotta learn to trust me."

She looked down. "I'm sorry," she said softly.

He lifted her chin and cradled it tenderly. "I only want what's best for you. You know that, don't you?"

"Yes," she said, gazing at him adoringly. "Yes, Hal. I do."

"Then, damn it! Trust me," he said sternly. His arms found the small of her back and drew her closer.

"I will."

"Good. Then do what I tell you from now on!"

***

One by one, almost everyone in Hal's study group exchanged wedding vows. Debbie married Ted, a burly sort of guy with a flamboyant persona. Most couples weren't really in love. They got married for the same reason they did everything else. They joined forces "because Hal said so." They didn't realize it yet, but those four words would become the doctrine under which they all would live.

Hal's followers had been married several months when he called them together for a special announcement.

"Edith and I found a huge house for rent," he said. "It's one of those old mansions on Thomas Road. If we pool our money, we can afford the rent. Who wants to join us?"

"Sounds good, but what about the island?" Frank asked.

"This doesn't mean I won't find us an island," he said. "Renting the mansion is only temporary."

Ellie didn't care if they ever moved to an island. She just wanted to be with Hal. Even though he sometimes treated her poorly, in a strange way, she was in love with him.

That was equally true for the other girls. They feared Hal, but at the same time, they loved him. Besides, even when he turned on them, he didn't stay angry long. His occasional outbursts seemed worth it for the over-the-top praise that was sure to follow. In their own way, the boys were also smitten. And as for Hal, the only thing he expected of his followers was to simply and blindly, follow his lead.

Ever since Nick and Ellie became husband and wife, they lived with Nick's mother, stepfather, and three brothers. The four boys had lost their father to a heart attack when Nick was a teenager. After their mother remarried, their stepfather let his wife continue to rule their household.

"Why couldn't you marry a nice Italian girl," Nick's mother asked more than once. "I think my handsome son could do better than Ellie. She's not Italian, and not even Catholic."

"Don't worry, Ma," he told her one afternoon. "I know it's crowded with us here, but we're gonna be leaving soon. We're moving into a mansion."

"A mansion? How you gonna afford a mansion?"

"Easy. Hal's arranged everything."

***

Not counting Hal and Edith, the mansion housed Nick and Ellie, Frank and Gloria, Charlie and Sonya, and two other couples. Most of the women were twenty-two; the men were two or three years older. Hal was thirty-five.

About seven months after move-in day, the first baby arrived ... right on their kitchen table. Hal didn't believe in doctors. Still, one was available for all deliveries.

First, Edith gave birth to Elizabeth. Then, six months later, Ellie delivered Gina. The following year Sonya had Dennis, Gloria had Larry, and Hal's only son, Carter, was born.

Life in the mansion wasn't perfect. The girls rotated cooking chores, which often led to small disputes. Hal couldn't be concerned with such trivial matters, and hearing about them made him livid. The girls quickly learned to keep such discussions out of his awareness.

After three years of communal living, Hal gathered his group together for some big news. However, when he stood in front of them, instead of appearing happy, his face was somber.

"Listen, I'm afraid I have rather sad news for you guys. I know I promised we'd be moving to an island," he said, his voice growing sadder. "But that's not going to be possible." Then he sat down, muttering how sorry he was.

His followers looked puzzled.

Minutes later, Hal broke into a grin. "Wait!" he said, standing up. "I can't keep torturing you guys. I'm sorry ... honest," he said chuckling. "I just couldn't help myself. Actually, I've got absolutely wonderful news for you." His voice burst with excitement. "How does living in the country, on over two hundred acres, sound to you guys?"

Having delivered the news, Hal promptly sat down.

Many questions followed: Where is it? How did you find it? When do we move?

Finally, Ellie asked what others were probably wondering. "Where in the world did you get the money to buy such a fabulous property?" Her inquiry was voiced before realizing that asking such a question might not be a good idea.

But Hal smiled warmly. "It's all thanks to Debbie," he said. He walked over and stood behind her. "Our good friend here put up all the money." He reached around and started stroking her upper arms.

"What? Wow!" Ellie exclaimed.

"Wow is right!" Hal said. "A friend of hers told her about the property. Then Debbie and I drove out to see it. And that, my friends, is all there was to it."

"Just like that?" Nick asked, smiling.

"Yep, just like that. And here's the best part. Debbie and Ted will finally be living with us. Isn't that wonderful?"

"I can't wait," Debbie said. "This will be the first time my money brought me any happiness."

Before the day ended, Hal revealed further information about the property. Their new home was located in the town of Cheltenham. It was a quaint community, with tiny shops in a four-block area. The purchase included several cows, a bull, goats, pigs, a rooster, and lots of chickens. There was one main farmhouse, a cottage, barn, shed, doghouse, chicken coop, and a granary. The property included an apple orchard, blackberry and raspberry bushes, gooseberries, currants, and plenty of room to grow vegetables. To Hal's followers, every detail sounded perfect.

During the coming weeks, Debbie and Ted often visited at the mansion to share in the excitement. For the most part, those two were exact opposites. Ted had been a football player in high school and everybody's friend. Debbie was introspective and reserved. But there was one thing they had in common ... their love for Hal.

One afternoon, while Ted helped the boys clean up the back yard, Debbie and the girls packed up belongings. Remembering a song she'd heard in a movie, Debbie started singing softly. With each verse, her voice got louder. On the next go-around, Ellie, Gloria, and Sonya joined in. A big theatrical finish brought their voices together in a makeshift harmony.

Edith shook her head as if to say that such foolishness was not for her.

In response, Sonya shouted, "One more time!"

The four girls sang the song again, even louder.

As moving day approached, Hal explained how they'd all be working together for the good of The Group. His plan allowed a few men to get outside jobs. But it was made abundantly clear that most of their income would be turned over to him. He would place it into a communal house fund.

Hal also pledged that after twenty years of loyal service, each couple would be awarded their own plot of land. The acreage was intended for their children to build houses for themselves.

"We'll all be joined together forever," he said.

Over time, Hal shared his list of rules. The most stringent one was the "no single folks" policy he had established for the island. However, since Rudy hap-pened to be single, and also happened to be the only one who knew anything about farming, that rule had to be changed. Hal's new law specified that only single wom-en would be banned.

Although the entire property had been purchased with Debbie's money, it seemed only fitting that Hal would make all the decisions and enforce all the rules.

And so he did.

CHAPTER 6

SPRING 1939 TO WINTER 1943

In the spring of 1939, unemployment in America was a little over seventeen percent. The minimum hourly wage was thirty cents per hour, and the average cost for a new house was $3,800. But for Hal and his followers, none of that mattered. For them a new beginning was on the horizon.

When moving day arrived, all members of The Group who owned any sort of jalopy filled it up at ten cents a gallon. Then they traveled, caravan-style, toward their personal Promised Land. Present were nine couples, five children, and their token experienced farmer, Rudy.

Despite limited belongings, Hal's followers had a plan, a dream, and a promise.

And they had Hal.

When Hal explained that only he knew what was best for them, turning away from family and friends seemed like a reasonable request. No one questioned why that rule didn't also apply to Hal's mother. She visited often, and Hal encouraged everyone to call her Mom.

And so they did.

***

Hal, Charlie, Sonya, Frank, Gloria, and most members of The Group were Jewish. Nick had been raised Catholic, and Ellie's parents were Christian Scientist. However, Hal influenced them all with his opinions about religion.

"Religion is just a crutch," he insisted. He also advised them to spare their children any religious upbringing. "Let them choose for themselves when they're older," he told them.

Hal's idea of a theology session often began with his personal interpretation of the Old Testament.

"In the beginning," he would preach in a voice that became explosive, "THERE WAS FEAR!"

And because his followers were convinced that Hal was the only one who could lead them to a happier life, they believed whatever he told them. In a sense, Hal was their god. Or so they were taught.

And so they believed.

***

Rudy, the only member of The Group with any farming skills, was among the first to move away. The others continued plowing the land, planting rows of corn, and bailing hay. However, slaughtering animals was more of a challenge. Nonetheless, Hal expected his community to be completely sustainable, so they had to try. After Rudy's departure, Hal placed Nick in charge of most farming endeavors.

One day, Nick hooked up a block and tackle to the side of the barn, creating a pulley with a rope threaded between. Then he hooked the loose end of the rope to the hind leg of a hog and dragged the animal up the barn wall while it screamed. The hog's front legs kicked so furiously that it was too dangerous to try and get a knife up against its throat. So Nick shot it. Then he and the other would-be farmers gutted and butchered it.

Since that worked out well, Hal decided that Nick should repeat the process with a cow. The next day, Nick led one of the cows toward the end of the rope. With one bullet to the brain, from a 22-caliber rifle, the animal jerked all four legs up into the air; then crashed heavily to the ground. After that, Nick attached the rope from the pulley to one of its legs. And with the aid of the strongest men (plus probably the horsepower of the tractor) they hauled it up the side of the barn.

For two days the dead cow was left hanging by one leg. At some point, one of the men slit the animal's throat to let the blood drain. Three days later the hanging carcass disappeared. On the fourth day, a delivery of neatly wrapped packages of steaks, roasts and ground beef arrived on The Farm. Apparently, the entire process of slaughtering cows was too involved for The Group. The local meat market was asked to intervene.

That was the end of Erehwon functioning as a self-sustainable community. Hal's followers continued to milk cows, raise chickens, gather eggs, and pick berries. They grew vegetables, froze and canned them. However, from then on, beef was purchased at the market.

Toward the end of their first month in the country, armed with a book filled with pictures and descriptions, Hal led several of his followers into the woods to search for wild mushrooms.

That evening, the woman assigned "cook of the day" tossed them into a soup. Thanks to Sonya, Charlie was the only adult who didn't get sick. The children were also spared; they weren't given the soup. Sonya was one of the few farmwomen who married for love, and just in case the wrong mushrooms had been picked, she kept her husband away from the table at suppertime. Sonya didn't want to eat the mushrooms, but in the end she did. She got violently ill along with the others.

Later, Hal was furious, demanding to know who had picked the mushrooms he tagged as poisonous. He was, after all, very knowledgeable about which plants were safe to eat.

So, notwithstanding the mushroom fiasco, and if you don't count the time Nick got badly stung during a bee-keeping disaster, Erehwon ran like a well-oiled John Deere.

***

Within two months of moving to the country Ellie's daughter, Kerri was born. She barely weighed four pounds at birth, but she was a fighter right from the start. Despite lack of follow-up medical care, Kerri grew into a healthy baby, full of vibrancy, sweetness, and smiles.

Kerri's older sister, Gina, had light brown hair. Freckles covered most of her face. Gina and Hal's daughter, Elizabeth, were close in age. They had fun playing together—unless of course, Elizabeth didn't get her way.

Those dynamics also held true during playtime with Dennis and Carter. Except that they didn't really enjoy playing together.

When it became obvious that Dennis (Charlie's son) could easily out-perform Carter (Hal's son) in various areas, Carter no longer wanted to interact with his cousin. Also, when Hal saw his son coming in second, it did not please him. And when Hal wasn't happy, anger followed. The relationship between Dennis and Carter became—shall we say—less than ideal.

About two and a half years after moving to The Farm, Sonya's son, Greg was born. Two days later, Ellie gave birth to Todd.

Shortly thereafter, Debbie found out that she was unable to conceive. After much consultation with Hal, she and Ted adopted four-year-old, Bobby, and his two-year-old sister, Janet.

Several years later, disaster struck.

A fire originating in the coal furnace, spread rapidly throughout the house. Hal and his followers formed a bucket brigade, and the Cheltenham volunteer firemen came to their aid. But it was too late. Their farmhouse burned to the ground. A few remaining buildings, including the cottage, chicken coop, and shed, had to accommodate over thirty-five people. Sheets and blankets, used as dividers, offered the only privacy between families. The men, plus two or three hired hands, worked night and day to build another home.

Because of heavy lifting associated with farming chores, Ellie had two miscarriages. She also delivered a stillborn baby boy. Then, in December of 1943, Ellie gave birth to her last child—a five pound, eight ounce baby girl. Nick and Ellie named her Anita, but everyone on The Farm knew her by her nickname. They called her Nita.

PART TWO

GROWING UP DIFFERENT

During a counseling session, I was advised to attend meetings for Adult Children of Alcoholics. This was suggested because, although my parents didn't have a drinking problem, their actions mimicked those who did. And it was true. They were addicted to Hal. They couldn't live without him. They compulsively sought his approval and seemed lost without his love.

> I need to set my secrets free.
> It's time, it's time ... come along with me.
> Join me, won't you? You just might say
> Good-bye to your own along the way.

Carter Darla Elizabeth Greg Todd Nita Gina Kerri Janet Ben Joey Dennis Julie Johnny Bobby Marty

The Farm kids, on the picnic table, in our front yard

Playing in the grass in our front yard - age three.

CHAPTER 7

MY FIRST MEMORY ...

I'm three years old and standing in our upstairs hall. Every light in the house must be on. Grown-ups are rushing past. Looks of panic fill their faces.

People are screaming.

Someone yells, "No!"

Someone else shrieks, "She's dead!"

The hall fills with mayhem. I feel scared.

I call out for my mother. No one seems to hear.

I see my father. He's shaking. An angry look covers his face.

Finally, I spot my mother. She's sitting on her bed.

Dad walks over, picks up a work shoe and hurls it violently through the window. Splinters of glass fly everywhere.

More yelling. More chaos.

My mother is bawling. She's hysterical.

"Debbie's dead! Debbie's dead!" she cries.

"I know ... I-I know," my father says. "I tried to tell Hal. I told him we should call a doctor."

That's all I remember from the night Debbie died. The next day all school-age children, even Debbie's kids, Bobby and Janet, attended classes as if nothing out of the ordinary had happened. That's how things played out on The Farm. Regardless of how traumatic an event was, or how devastating the circumstances, we had to numb it all out. Nothing was explained, and all our feelings remained unacknowledged.

CHAPTER 8

*B*lended families are quite common today, and a multitude of variations make up a family. However, in the 1940's and 1950's (at least where I grew up), a family consisted of a mother, a father, and their children. Occasionally, grandparents also lived with the immediate family.

If there were other communes or cults anywhere near the town where I lived, they were certainly unknown to me. I felt like we were the only people in the whole world who lived like we did.

When I was five and a half, I recall posing for a photograph with my brother and sisters. Mom had placed Kerri (age 10) and Todd (age 8) on opposite ends of our couch. Gina (age 12) sat in the center with me, pretending to read me a book. (See photo insert.)

After the moment was captured on film, I asked Mom why the picture was taken. My mother looked slightly annoyed and somewhat puzzled, as if the answer should have been obvious.

"Because this is your family," she said emphatically.

It is? Who knew? There were a dozen other kids playing in the next room.

Living with so many people was the easy piece to a very complicated equation. At the pinnacle of feeling different was this fact: The children of Erehwon were, in essence, turned over to Hal. We were raised as he saw fit. However, that disadvantage didn't come with any special privilege. Such preferential treatment was reserved for the resident three brats—Hal's true offspring.

Elizabeth was his firstborn. Although she was a mere six months older than my sister, Gina, she held the distinction of oldest kid on The Farm. Their son, Carter, was similar in age to Charlie's son, Dennis. Their baby girl, Darla, was 8 months younger than me.

All kids on The Farm were subject to a "comparison game" of sorts with Hal's *perfect* children. This was especially true for those similar in age. Gina was compared to Elizabeth, Dennis to Carter, and me to Darla.

Consequently, some of us developed some well-founded fears of not quite measuring up. To make matters more unbearable, all the grown-ups seemed to prefer Hal's kids to their own.

Simply put, Hal's children were royalty. Compared to them, we were children with faces pressed to the candy store window. We could see all the treats on the other side, but knew that none of them were for us.

Children of the king shouldn't do chores, right?

Hal and Edith didn't think so either.

The rest of us had never-ending tasks like changing the rabbits' cages, a particularly pungent ordeal. We'd get chased by Bossy the cow and charged by nasty, smelly Victor the goat.

My favorite task was feeding garbage to the pen full of pigs. One time, I claimed a little piglet as my own and named her Polka Dot. I don't recall exactly where I got that name or precisely when she ended up on our supper table.

We fed hay to the horses, saving some for the strawberry plants to protect the berries from getting crushed into the dirt. Later, we picked those berries (one for the basket and one for me). Then they got washed, hulled, and made into jam.

We also picked raspberries, blackberries, currants, and gooseberries, plus a few varieties I've probably forgotten. We milked cows on three legged stools and drank the frothy milk right from the bucket. The cream got separated and butter was churned. Eggs were gathered from hundreds of chickens. Whenever fried chicken was on the menu, we'd stand mesmerized while watching them run around without any heads, their blood spurting out everywhere.

Still, our lifestyle wasn't all work and chores. Neither was it total fun and games. The dynamics were rather complicated. For one thing, communicating affection was nowhere to be found or felt. Hal had some rather strange psychological ideas. Perhaps he believed that showing affection would cause weakness. I understand that when Carter was seven or eight, Hal took him aside. Then he'd tell everyone he didn't want to be disturbed. His son would look up in terror as our leader led him into the library. Hal told the others he was teaching Carter to be a leader among men. Heaven only knows what went on behind that closed door.

And where was the love? I don't recall hearing my parents, or anyone else, utter the words, "I love you." Nor do I recall any positive words flowing *from* anyone *to* anyone. That was probably because love was not the bond that brought most of these couples together. The majority of Hal's followers joined forces for one reason only. They got married "because Hal said so." That little catchphrase became their incentive for just about everything.

From Singer's *Cults in Our Midst* (258):

"Children see no modeling of compassion, forgiveness, kindness or warmth in cults. Since all members are expected to idolize the leader, so are the children. Children either identify with the leader's power and dominance or capitulate and become passive, dependent, obedient, and often emotionally subdued and flattened."

CHAPTER 9

Every creek, wooded area, and building on The Farm was given a name. The Big House, where most of the families lived, was the largest home on our property. The cooking, canning, eating, and group sessions with Hal occurred here.

The house wasn't much to look at. The two-story dwelling turned a dismal gray when the white paint chipped away. Upstairs there were three bedrooms, a bathroom, and hall. The downstairs featured a huge kitchen, large living room, dining room, and a small library. A coatroom was attached to the front door. The back entrance had a filthy screen door with millions of tiny fingerprints. Our front and back doors were never locked. During my childhood (spanning the early 1940's to mid 1950's), fears of outside threats were seldom a concern in rural Ohio.

Three tall maple trees lined the front yard of the Big House. In autumn, mountainous piles of big golden leaves provided hours of fun. In early spring, buckets hung from those trees. The sap was collected and boiled down to make maple syrup. But it was a much more complicated operation than that. Not the least of which involved a sleigh and two enormous Belgium workhorses.

Lady-Bell and Lindy-Bell were so powerfully built that I'm sure they could have leveled the barn if Hal issued the command. However, our leader had another use for those horses—like pulling a sleigh full of grownups and older kids (led by my father) into a forest of maple trees.

When the leaves turned glorious shades of red and yellow, that scene resembled a New England landscape transported to Ohio. During heavy snowfalls, that wooded area became a winter wonderland. Finally, after the weather turned warmer, it was sugaring time.

Then it was over the Driveway Creek and through Seven Dwarfs Forest, to the Sugar Shanty we'd go. Most days, the water level of that creek was extremely low. The sleigh made the crossing without difficulty. However, when the snow melted, it became a slightly deeper body of water. Then, to avoid getting splashed, the kids had to climb onto the backs of those massive horses and hang on tight. Fearful, they held their breath until safely back in the sleigh.

Once in Seven Dwarfs Forest, the adults and kids would drill waist-high holes into each tree. Then they'd drive a hollow wooden peg (spigot) into the hole. From it they hung a bucket to collect the sap as it dripped. As the buckets filled up with sap, it was collected and poured into a huge galvanized tank attached to the sleigh.

When all the buckets were emptied, or the tank was full, Dad led the workhorses to the Sugar Shanty. There, the sap was poured onto a huge metal container. A fire was built underneath. When the sap threatened to boil over, my father threw in a small amount of butter. As the butter melted and spread over the surface, it quieted the boiling sap. Then, after it cooked quite a long while, voila ... maple syrup.

Even though the Sugar Shanty was a small one-story building, I thought it was enormous when I first saw it. Maybe that was due to the blazing fire that lit up the place. Or perhaps it only seemed bigger because I was five at the time.

I remember my first trip to the shanty like this ...

My brother and I were playing by the shed. Todd missed his opportunity to catch a ride with Dad on the sleigh. I was too young to go sugaring, but Todd wasn't. Not wanting to miss out on the fun, he decided to walk the distance.

When Todd took off for the forest, I tagged along. I had to. I was afraid I'd never find our house by myself. Todd kept pointing the way, but I ignored him.

"Okay," he said, groaning. "Come on, I'll take you with me."

Everything went well until we reached the Driveway Creek. Todd picked up a thick tree branch and plopped it over the water.

"Come on," he said. "You can do it. I'll hold the branch for you."

I managed to get halfway across before landing ankle-deep in the freezing water.

"Oh no! Now you've done it!" Todd yelled. "I told you to go home!"

I started to cry, but kept walking. I couldn't lose Todd now. I'd surely never find my way back to the Big House.

How we reached the front door of the Sugar Shanty I'll never understand. We arrived freezing cold and eager to warm ourselves by the fire. But such pleasures were quickly interrupted by Mom's fury. She screamed at us, saying we shouldn't have come.

Gee, ya think? And who was watching us to prevent that from happening? I felt bad for Todd. He received most of Mom's wrath that day. He tried to get me to turn around. But I was afraid that I'd never find our house. Hey, I was five!

CHAPTER 10

In our front yard we had two of the best swings any kid could ever want. My father, and other men on the farm, crafted them. First, they secured a huge plank across two maple trees. Then they drilled holes into wooden boards and tied hanging ropes underneath. Those swings went up so high; one of the older boys was convinced that if he got up high enough and took a leap, he could fly. Poor Superman. He landed in the ditch with a broken arm.

Six evergreens lined the entrance of our circular asphalt driveway. Our leader spoke of placing Santa and his reindeer atop those trees for the Christmas season. But that never happened.

Growing along the side of the Big House were two Snowball bushes. One was pure white and the other a pale pink. In the spring, lovely lilacs, smelling as sweet as a rose with a hint of vanilla, bloomed beside our well. Near the field where we played baseball, an elderberry bush produced dark purple clusters of berries that grew like grapes on a vine.

"Elderberry fight," one of the kids would holler. Within minutes, we grabbed handfuls, chose sides and threw them, allowing the purple clumps to splatter everywhere. We'd return home with stained shirts and faces but never got into trouble. I doubt that any of the grown-ups noticed. We were usually left to care for ourselves, with little, if any, adult supervision.

Before I was born, a one-room schoolhouse was transported to our property. It was placed atop a foundation across the circular driveway from the Big House. It came equipped with a blackboard (complete with pull-down maps) and a potbellied stove. In time, the blackboard was transferred to the basement of the Big House, the relic stove discarded, and a second story (with bathroom) added. Naturally, it was always called the School House. Hey, I never said we were original—or even very clever—only that we named everything.

A cottage, which came with the property, was torn down during my early years. It was replaced with a tiny, boxy-looking house that had been a prototype for inexpensive homes after the war. That structure was plopped down on a foundation on the other side of the Big House. A field of clover (also known as our baseball diamond) separated those two houses. Because the exterior, roof, and interior walls of the smaller home were thin sheets of steel, we always referred to it as, yep—you guessed it—the Steel House.

The Steel House was where Hal's brother, Charlie, and his family slept. I always liked Charlie. He was a lot different from Hal. In fact, it was years before I realized that they were brothers. The two men were about as much alike as Laurel and Hardy.

Hal was short (about five foot six inches), built rather round, and not very attractive. Charlie, ten years younger, was tall, had a kind smile, and an excellent physique. And here's something else. While Hal was loud and acted like a know-it-all, Charlie had a reserved, easy-going manner. Like I said, Laurel and Hardy.

I often thought Hal was like a two-sided monster. Oops, I meant to say coin. One side represented a fatherly image, known to enjoy planning birthday parties and making people feel special. The flip side revealed a hideous beast with a giant foot that hovered over tiny ants. Heads, you win. Tails, you're squished.

Still, to our leader's credit, the man was loaded with charisma. Or so everyone else seemed to think. And I suppose it was true. Otherwise, why would all the grown-ups gaze at him with adoring eyes, following after him like a dog in heat ... hoping for a few kernels of insight?

Personally, I never understood how anyone with a facial mole the size of a peanut, appeared to have swallowed a watermelon, and ran around screaming, "You're nothing but a bunch of hypocrites," could be considered charming or captivating. Ah well, I had a lot to learn about personal magnetism and sex appeal.

From Singer's *Cults in Our Midst* (8):

"Cult leaders tend to be determined and domineering and are often described as charismatic. These leaders need to have enough personal drive, charm, or other pulling power to attract, control, and manipulate their flock."

***

Hal's brother, Charlie, was married to Sonya, a petite woman with a rather spunky personality. In my younger years, Charlie and Sonya had three boys and a girl. Although their family slept in the Steel House, they joined us in the Big House for meals, sessions with Hal, playtime, chores, and almost everything else. In those days, the Steel House served only as a place to sleep.

From what I've heard, when Hal and his followers first moved to the country, everything was great fun. They performed difficult chores, requiring long hours. But everyone pitched in. They were a team. A family.

However, after a few years of struggling, Hal realized it took more than hard labor to run a farm. Glenwood Photography Studio (The Studio, as it was called) was purchased to help subsidize their farming venture. It specialized in wedding, bar mitzvah, confirmation, and graduation class photographs.

The purchase of The Studio was Hal's brother's cue to trade in his overalls for a business suit and camera. Before long, my mother joined him. Apparently, Hal decided that she was a terrible mother and my siblings and I would be better off without her. Mom's new job involved posing the wedding parties, playing receptionist, and using oil paints to turn black and white photos into beautiful color portraits. Her jack-of-all-trades position was performed with very little pay. That's right. Both Charlie and Mom worked for practically nothing. It was all part of Hal's Master Plan. And no one (at least in the beginning) wanted it any other way.

Once Mom started working at The Studio, my father found a job in the city as well. Almost all of his salary was likewise deposited into Hal's communal house fund. But they were an "all for one/one for all" team. So, I suppose that made perfect sense.

Being the third youngest kid on The Farm, I was dubbed one of the Three Babies. That little trio also included Hal's youngest daughter, Darla, and Charlie's youngest son, Joey. All others were known as the Big Kids.

All kids, big and little, played in Snail Woods, Seven Dwarfs Forest, Bee Sting Creek, The Driveway Creek, The Creek, and The Lagoon. Our property comprised roughly 225 acres, and the kids roamed wild and free over the entire place—mostly without supervision.

Sounds like fun, doesn't it? It was.

Sometimes.

CHAPTER 11

Feelings of being different first crept into my aware-ness when a classmate of one of the Big Kids asked, "If you guys aren't related, why do you all live together?"

Upon hearing that, I decided right then and there, I was *never* going to school. However, while watching the Big Kids line up for the school bus, I must have appeared eager to join them.

"Don't worry, Nita," I heard Hal's wife, Edith, say in her sickening-sweet voice I'd grown to hate. "You can go with them next year."

As usual, the woman couldn't have been further off base. I hoped to never, ever, join that line-up. Our lead-er's wife was one of the more nondescript farmwomen. She had black curly hair and a rather pretty face. But the woman was painfully quiet. When she did utter a word or two, it was usually something I didn't want to hear.

School wasn't the only thing I feared. I never wanted to grow up, period. That concept filled me with pure terror. The reason was simple. Growing up would turn me into one of *them*. I'd seen how badly the mothers were treated. I wanted none of that.

The realization that our lifestyle was nowhere near normal turned personal about six months before I began first grade. The afternoon started out rather exciting. I had never left The Farm before. So when Dad asked me to go with him to borrow some tools, I was thrilled.

Our neighbor had a daughter a year younger than me. We played together while our fathers talked about screwdrivers, or whatever it was they were discussing. Sally showed me her room, we played with her dolls, and her mother offered peanut butter and jelly sandwiches.

On one hand, that afternoon was a lot of fun. However, measured on the "being different" scale, visiting Sally only amplified the vast differences between "us" and "them." And by "them," I mean the rest of the world.

For one thing, where were the other mothers, or the dozens of children hiding? Who was their leader? And where did Sally's father kill the rabbits? At home that deed was done in our cellar.

The other kids and I would line our basement steps. We watched, in morbid fascination, as my father pulled the helpless rabbits from their holding cell and spun them around until their necks snapped. He'd skin them; then cut each one into tiny pieces. We didn't leave until all the skins were hanging on the clothesline above our wringer-washer. I didn't want to see the whole gory scene but couldn't look away.

Thinking back on all that, I'm struck with how much the women on The Farm were like those scared rabbits, each waiting their turn to be cornered and skinned alive by Hal.

CHAPTER 12

*J*ust as I watched the gruesome action on the basement steps with the other farm kids, there were times
when we witnessed Hal emotionally slicing and dicing our
mothers. I remember one such time like this ...

I was positioned in the doorway separating our dining
room and kitchen. As usual, the kids were fed first. Then
the grown-ups enjoyed a leisurely supper, followed by
a night of socializing. Although Hal's teachings focused
on adult topics, having children present was neither forbidden nor discouraged. In fact, Hal would often parade
his own children before The Group, bragging about how
wonderful they were.

Hal's so-called teaching sessions often ended with him slamming down the book he was analyzing and screaming, "You guys are nothing but a bunch of hypocrites!"

I had no idea what that word meant, but knew it couldn't be good. Otherwise, why would he storm from the room like a mad man afterward?

That night, instead of the usual book discussion, music filled the room. Louis Armstrong had a distinctive way of delivering a song, and watching Hal imitate his unique singing style was quite entertaining.

It wasn't long before the other grown-ups joined him in doing their best "Satchmo" imitation. Well, everyone that is, except Charlie's wife, Sonya. She sat alone in the corner, tapping her foot to the music.

Hal walked over to her.

"C'mon, Sonya ... sing with me," Hal said, smiling at her.

"Oh, Hal, I can't sing. I'd rather listen to you guys."

She was right. She didn't have much of a singing voice. Dancing was her specialty.

"Nonsense! Sure you can sing. Everyone can sing. C'mon, I'll teach ya," he said, coaxing her toward the middle of the room.

As the two of them sang, Sonya added little soft shoe dance steps. At some point, most grown-ups started clapping hands and stomping feet. That was when Hal stopped singing.

He stood motionless, staring intently at his followers.

When the record ended, cheers went out for Sonya to keep dancing. However, Hal had another plan. Like pressing the eject button and informing them it was time for bed.

"Hey, c'mon," my mother protested. "It's early. We're only getting started here."

"Oh! So you think we should stay up, do you?" Hal said. "And who just died and made you boss?"

He pulled his record off the turntable and stared disapprovingly at the others.

"Well, what are you guys waiting for?" he said. "I told you to go to bed. So go already!"

No one dared to move.

"Okay," he said, his voice dripping with sarcasm. "Ellie, since you're so keen on staying up, that's what we'll do. Let's stay up!"

"N-no, you're right. It's l-late," my mother stammered. "We really should go to bed."

Hal's tirade seemed endless. First, he listed all the things Mom wasn't doing right in general. Then he switched to what had to be his favorite topic—what a lousy mother she was.

It wasn't unusual to see Hal chastising the women. I'd seen the "hot seat" procedure many times, with one mother or another. Our fathers had to follow Hal's commands, but it was the women who were treated with the most disdain.

It pained me to watch Mom taking Hal's assault. I wanted to pull her out of the room. I wanted to scream at Hal. But, like all of those controlled by that man, I sat stiff and silent, careful not to breathe too loud.

Finally, as if he had just delivered a well-received discourse, the King of the Big House promptly left the room.

The party was over.

From Singer's *Cults in Our Midst* (75):

"Many groups use a 'hot seat' technique or some other form of criticism to attain the goal of undercutting, destabilizing, and diminishing."

CHAPTER 13

Certainly not every element of my childhood was un-happy. After all, I had creeks to swim in and caves to explore. I swung on monkey vines, ran barefoot through fields of clover, picked buttercups, bluebells, and other wildflowers. I played baseball, kickball, kick-the-can, and caught lightning bugs in Mason jars; all rather normal goings on for country kids during the 1940's and 1950's. However, trauma was never far away. Hal's nephew, Greg, found that out after a simple game of baseball ...

GREG'S STORY

Charlie's son, Greg, was an extremely intelligent kid with a creative sense of humor. He even invented a story about the color of his hair.

"I got it from my mother," he'd insist.

Not from Sonya's flaming red locks, but rather from diving into The Creek, cracking his head open on a rock, and having his mom treat the wound. And I had no reason to doubt him. The blood-red bottle of Mercurochrome, used for treating cuts, always stained our skin and clothes ... so why not hair?

Greg was Todd's age. Their birthdays were only days apart. They loved playing baseball almost as much as listening to Jimmy Dudley call the Cleveland Indians play-by-plays on the radio.

"It's a long line drive, going out into center field. Giordano's under it and he makes the catch," my brother would shout before capturing the ball in his glove.

Still, there were days when everything went terribly wrong. Like the time Greg accidentally hit one of the girls with a baseball.

Someone on her team got angry and yelled out the dreaded warning all kids on The Farm feared.

"You're gonna be sorry. I'm telling Hal!"

"C'mon. I didn't mean it," Greg said. "Anyway, she's fine now."

But Greg's logic failed to stop the inevitable.

After supper, several kids were running through the front yard playing tag. Suddenly the screen door burst wide open. Within seconds Hal came charging across the yard like a bull released from its pen.

Without saying a word, eyes glaring, Hal stopped in front of Greg. He raised a hand and slapped his nephew across the face with such force it knocked him to the ground.

Every kid looked fearful that they might be next.

Hal sneered at Greg stretched out on the ground. "Let that be a lesson for the rest of you!" he bellowed before storming away.

Tears welled up in Greg's eyes. He had received quite a blow, both physically and emotionally. However, soon he was back in the Big House playing games and acting like nothing at all had happened.

Greg never mentioned the incident to his parents, and they never brought it up to him. That's the way it was on The Farm. Hal was The Boss and could do whatever he wanted, to whomever he wanted, and whenever he pleased.

CHAPTER 14

*I*n the early days, children as young as three gathered around the potbellied stove in the School House for instructions about how to live according to Hal. On Christmas morning, those lessons were taught by example.

None of the other parents were allowed to be there or to distribute any presents. That was Hal's big show. But he didn't play Santa Claus for every child. If he happened to be annoyed with a particular kid, or with a child's parents, that kid was passed over. Then they had to quietly watch as the ones deemed "good enough" opened their gifts.

Our leader's actions, teetering from kind to cruel, showed up in numerous ways ...

JULIE'S STORY

Charlie and Sonya's only daughter was a quiet child. She had her mother's big brown eyes and her father's gentle nature. Her persona, although shy, was sweet and innocent.

As second grade began for Julie, Hal presented her with a list of school supplies. He instructed her to take it to her mother. The next day, Julie was in the yard of the Big House playing dolls with Kerri.

Hal cheerfully strolled over.

"Hi, honey. Did you give your mom the list?" he asked. "Did she need to add anything?"

"List? What list?" Julie asked, barely looking up.

"You remember, honey," he said, filled with warmth and affection. "The list of school supplies. Remember?" he said smiling.

"Oh, that. I left it in my room. Be right back," she said before darting off to go home.

Unfortunately, Julie had forgotten to show her mother the list and had no idea where it was. Upon returning to the Steel House, Julie searched and searched. Finally, she had to go back to Hal and admit the truth.

"What?" Hal blasted back. "You lost it? Well, you'd better go find it. Understand?"

"But I searched everywhere, Uncle Hal," she said fearfully. "I don't know where it is. "I'm sorry."

"You're sorry? You're sorry!" he screamed. "What good is that? Being sorry won't bring that list back, now will it?"

While Hal was technically Julie's uncle, she was well aware that he wielded his power over everyone. Her body trembled.

"That won't do, little girl," Hal said, with a sinister sneer. "I try to teach you responsibility, and all you can do is stand there shaking like a fool. Perhaps I'm not making myself clear." He grasped her tiny chin in his big hand and glared into her eyes. "Or maybe you don't want to learn responsibility. Maybe all you care about is playing with dolls."

Then he softened his tone. A warm expression filled his face. "Don't you see, Julie?" he said, lovingly. "I'm only trying to help you." Then he squeezed her chin a little too hard before abruptly letting go.

Julie could barely breathe. "I'll find it; I promise," she said, running away in tears.

"Well, you'd better!" Hal shouted, his voice escalating with each word, "Because if I find it ... I'm gonna shove it down your throat!"

Frightened and trembling, Julie dashed home.

Sonya was in the back yard hanging clothes. Julie rushed to her side. "Mom ... Mom ... he yelled at me," Julie said, clutching her mother's leg. Her body quivered. Her words came out short and choppy. "I'm scared," she said. "I'm so scared."

Sonya slipped a clothespin through the towel she was hanging. Then she stooped down to her child's level. "Who yelled at you, Julie? Who was it?"

"Uncle Hal! It was Uncle Hal. He got so mad at me."

"What?" Sonya said, her voice turning angry. "Why? What did you do?"

"I lost the list," she said, clinging tighter to her mother.

"What list? Julie, what are you talking about?"

"The school supply list. I was supposed to bring it home. And I did. I brought it home to show you. But then I forgot to give it to you. And now ... now I can't find it anywhere."

Sonya's eyes widened. She pulled away from her daughter. Her arms crossed over her chest. "How could you?" she shrieked.

"I'm sorry, Mom. Honest, I didn't mean to—"

"Julie, why cantcha ever do as you're told?"

"I know. I'm sorry. But Mom, he got so mad at me."

"Well, of course he got mad," Sonya shot back. "That list was important. What did you expect?"

"But Mom, I'm so scared. He told me if I don't find it, he would. And when he finds it," she said sobbing. "Oh Mom … when he finds it, he's gonna shove it down my throat."

"Yeah," her mother screamed. "Well, I'm gonna help him!"

From Singer's *Cults in Our Midst* (256):

"Moreover, anger and frustration is engendered in the parents by the cult leader's actions, but because they dare not express this anger toward him, when they do see their children they often act out their anger on their children instead."

Julie's story shows how a mother's natural instinct to protect her children can be temporarily altered under the influence of a domineering cult leader who exercises power cruelly and unjustly. Sonya was one of the most loving mothers on The Farm. Yet, even she was caught in Hal's web of psychological abuse. I feel certain that Sonya's anger was linked to a well-founded fear. She was probably afraid of what might happen to her because of her child's less than perfect actions.

CHAPTER 15

I didn't want to start school. I was afraid about what would happen when I tried to fit in with the outside world. I hoped that day would never come. But sure enough, in September of 1949, it came anyway.

Mrs. Carlton had worked at our public school for years. She taught first grade to all kids on The Farm. When my turn came, the woman was probably no older than forty-five, but her salt and pepper hair made her look ancient.

During the first hour of school my class was divided into three circles. Seven or eight kids were in each group. My teacher distributed pencils and paper; then presented a rather simple assignment.

"Write out your first name," she told us. "When you're done, you may return to your desk."

That was easy. Kerri had been teaching me to print before I started school. I quickly turned in my paper with a proud grin.

However, my teacher's reaction surprised me.

"No, I'm sorry. That's not right," she said. "Try again."

Not right? What's she talking about? I knew it was right.

I made sure that my next efforts were neater. Nonetheless, her response remained the same. On my third attempt she offered a hint.

"You're forgetting the 'A' at the beginning of your name," she said with a smile.

I was pretty sure she was wrong. But adding it was my only hope of re-joining my classmates. To my delight, it worked.

Our next task was reciting The Lord's Prayer.

What Lord's Prayer? What's she talking about now?

When my classmates stood up, my feet hit the floor. When they lowered their heads, mine went down, too.

Then the mumbling began. I had no idea what was going on. We didn't pray at home. Hal said religion was a crutch. Would this never end?

After what felt like an hour had passed, everyone murmured a word I'd later learn was "amen." Then everyone sat down. Finally!

When Mrs. Carlton spoke, my classmates seemed to listen intently. I didn't. My mind was stuck on thoughts like: Is everyone looking at me? Do they know about The Farm? Could they tell I didn't know the prayer? Do they think I'm different?

Soon my teacher announced recess.

There were two girls, Pam and Nancy, who most girls seemed to naturally gravitate toward. It didn't take long to realize that those two were the "it girls" of first grade. Both had Shirley Temple curls. Nancy's were light brown, and Pam's a honey-blond.

During recess they spun 'round and 'round. Their ringlets danced with each twirl; their skirts flared further out with every turn. Before the bell rang, Nancy issued her number one "in crowd" rule: Only girls with full skirts would be allowed in their circle the next day.

The following morning I woke up early. I needed to catch my mother before she left for work. For openers, I had to uncover the mystery behind the missing letter in my name.

Turns out, my teacher was right. Apparently, Nita was my nickname. The "A" *did* belong before the "N." Who knew?

My mother also taught me enough of The Lord's Prayer so I could fake it. And best of all, she found a skirt that swirled softly as I spun around. Perhaps it didn't flare out quite as far as I'd wanted. Still, things were beginning to look promising.

I went to school firmly believing I had the winning ticket past Nancy's coveted gates of acceptance. But wait! Not so fast, Nita with an "A." Tuesday wasn't full skirt day.

By afternoon, another problem was percolating. Somehow the lunch conversation shifted to birthdays and what month everyone had turned six. Oops, I was only five. When Nancy found that out, she sternly informed me that I had no business being in school.

"Go home and don't come back until you're six," she commanded.

The next morning I relayed Nancy's demands to Mom, secretly hoping she'd keep me home for another year. Too bad my mother didn't fear Nancy like I did.

"You'll be six in three months," she told me. "Don't worry about it. It's perfectly fine."

Easy for her to say; not exactly what I wanted to hear.

That morning, while boarding the school bus, I wondered how long it would be before Nancy reminded me that I didn't belong.

CHAPTER 16

Two Lassie look-alikes also called The Farm home. Both were sable and white purebred collies. Casey, the female, was the most serene. Although I won't say she was completely passive, she could usually be found sleeping under the lilac bush the entire day.

Cody was the noble sire. He had a muscular body with a beautiful, thick undercoat of fur. Those two were an unbeatable combination, creating litter after litter of adorable puppies. Four weeks after birth, Edith would erect a sign, letting passer-bys know that pedigree collie pups were available for a price.

Casey was usually a terrific mother. But during the summer that Kerri turned ten and I was six, she ignored one of her pups. When Casey refused to nurse her, Kerri used a tiny eyedropper to administer the nourishment.

She tended to the early morning, mid-afternoon, and even middle of the night feedings. Yet, no matter how hard Kerri tried, the pup often turned her head away. That's when my sister would cuddle her and said, "Don't worry, Ginger. It's okay if you don't feel like eating. I'll come back later. Maybe you'll be hungry then."

Despite Kerri's best efforts, Ginger remained the runt of the litter. When it became apparent that Edith couldn't sell her, Kerri begged to keep Ginger as a pet. Finally, Edith gave in.

While, technically, Ginger belonged to Kerri, I loved her, too. I even made up stories based on whatever mischief I could conjure up for her to experience. I called them *The Adventures of Ginger-Cake and Sally* and shared them with anyone who sat long enough to listen.

Ginger had the sweet disposition of Casey plus the beauty of Cody. Over the years we had several dogs. However, Ginger, that "too cute for words" collie, was the only one I truly loved.

CHAPTER 17

Second grade didn't begin well for me. I was sitting at my desk a short while when Mrs. Carlton walked in clutching a piece of paper. She held it up and proceeded to read off names. Pam, my favorite friend from first grade, heard her name called. So did Nancy. I watched as one student after another disappeared out the door. I had no idea what was going on, but one thing was certain: If Pam and Nancy were leaving; I wanted my name on that list, too. But it wasn't.

Mrs. Carlton informed us that the students who left the room would be sharing space with third graders. One breath later, she let us know that since our names hadn't been called, we would remain where we were—in the first grade classroom.

I glanced around. Sally, the girl I played with when Dad borrowed tools, was sitting next to Darla. Both had started first grade. While it was nice seeing Sally again, without Pam and Nancy I knew second grade wouldn't be much fun. And it wasn't.

I frequently got into trouble for disruptive behavior like talking in class, or turning wads of paper into rockets launched across the classroom.

During that entire school year, my anger was usually on the verge of erupting. Consequently, I kept my teacher busy dishing out punishments like putting me in the corner at recess. I didn't care. I had good reason to be angry. My name should have been on that stupid list!

Nevertheless, during that school year I did experience a few amusing moments. The funniest was when Todd, Kerri, and I dressed up for our school's annual Halloween contest.

Kerri chose an ugly witch's mask with a crooked nose and protruding wart. To compliment it, she wore one of Mom's old housedresses. It was strategically padded to create an extra large bosom and rear end. If that wasn't silly enough, she held a long elegant cigarette holder, as if she were a member of New York's high society. The total effect transformed my sister into the funniest fat momma this side of Ma Kettle.

Todd sported extra large coveralls, stuffed with old rags. His padding made him appear to be over two hundred pounds. A pair of too-big-for-him clodhoppers turned him into an obese farmer preparing to plow the fields.

My get-up was much less involved. It consisted of a diaper, bonnet, and baby bottle.

We had fun creating those costumes, but I never thought we'd win. Boy, was I wrong. As masks were removed, I heard the judges chanting what would become a familiar refrain:

"Why, it's the Giordano Funny Family!"

With those costumes we stole the show two years in a row.

CHAPTER 18

The way Hal and Edith's kids strutted around, you'd think they were part of the British Royal Family. Why not? That's how they were treated.

Their youngest daughter, Darla, was a slightly pudgy, brown-eyed child with short, dark wavy hair. She was often given special gifts, like the beautiful coat with matching fur muff presented to her when she was five. I'd tell you they weren't any nicer than the hand-me-down jackets and holes-in-the-fingers gloves the rest of us wore, but then I'd just be lying.

Their oldest child, Elizabeth, had a slim figure, smooth, jet-black hair and a pretty face. She would have been attractive if not for her air of superiority that blew all those physical attributes into the next county. I remember how that attitude came shining through when her father brought home a, loaded to the brim, foot high Dan Dee potato chip can. Do you think she'd offer any to us mere commoners while she lounged around munching away? Yeah, right!

Elizabeth's "better than you" attitude came out in numerous ways. Like the time she swiped my breakfast off the counter with a snotty, "Oh, thank you. That looks good!"

'Make your own darn breakfast,' I wanted to tell her. 'Get off your lazy butt and fry your own bacon and eggs,' I wanted to scream.

But I didn't dare. What I did was shove the stool back under the broiler, grab a frying pan, and start over.

Their middle child, Carter, was a lanky kid who seemed to love strutting around like the heir apparent. More than once I wanted to knock him off his high and mighty throne, especially when he pointed his beloved BB gun at us. Naturally, none of the grown-ups ever attempted to stop him. He was, after all, Hal's only son. I suppose that meant if he blinded one of us, then so be it.

The day came when Hal's sister-in-law, Sonya, took issue with such favoritism. But before that happened, she dared to disagree with Hal about one of his rules.

Following an angry exchange of words, Hal informed her, "If you don't like the way I run things, you can take your family and go live in the Steel House ... and don't come back."

Yep, that's right. Hal banned his own brother and family from the Big House. They didn't eat supper with us and were no longer welcome at Hal's evening sessions. To my way of thinking, the fact that they had their own home, and didn't have to adhere to Hal's rules, was a lucky break. However, being forbidden to walk through our doors carried a certain sense of shame.

Still, their children were permitted to play anywhere outside. So, while we planted our enormous garden, their five-year-old, Joey, stood by with a jealous eye. Before long his mother was helping him cultivate a small patch of ground a few yards from our corn, cucumbers, carrots, lettuce and other salad fixings.

About harvesting time, Carter took notice. "Hey, Joey, you can't have a garden here," he called out from his tractor seat, his black hair blowing in the breeze. "You can plant one by the Steel House, but not here!" he hollered. Then he proceeded to plow up Joey's garden.

In response, Joey tore across the Big House lawn and baseball field, reaching his house in record time.

Within minutes, a furious-looking Sonya was on the scene. She seemed ready to give Carter a one-two punch he'd never forget. And she almost did.

Their confrontation began with a rather heated debate. Following a few nasty words, Sonya pulled Carter off that John Deere and into the dirt. The battle didn't end until they both rolled over several times, landing in the ditch alongside the highway.

I'm not sure if Joey ever planted another garden, but I do know that was the first time I ever witnessed a mother standing up for her child. What a beautiful sight! Sonya was my hero.

CHAPTER 19

*A*s the years passed, I learned the origin of the fire I saw ignited within Sonya that day ...

SONYA'S STORY – AGE NINETEEN

Sonya Goldstein was an aspiring dancer and new to the ways of New York City. It was a little past eight A.M. The beeping and clanging sounds of the city let her know that it was time for the day to begin.

Some people back home suggested that Sonya wasn't tall enough to become a dancer. She only stood five feet tall. But Sonya didn't concern herself with such nonsense.

"Jerry will be calling today," she said. "I know it. And when he does, I'll be ready."

She said those same words every morning since the bus driver dropped her off at the terminal.

Sonya glanced around her pay-by-the-week rooming house. The place was a bit run down. Still, it was right where she needed to be—near Times Square and the hub of the Broadway Theater District.

Before leaving home, she told her Aunt Sarah, "I can't be spending money on cab fares. Besides, I want to be close to the action; ready and waiting for whenever Jerry calls."

Checking herself in the full-length mirror, Sonya ran fingers through her hair. "Oh, it's so fine ... too fine," she said. "Why didn't I get Daddy's hair?" Looking at her legs, she smiled. "Oh, that's okay ... no one's gonna be noticing my hair when I'm dancing on Broadway. I guess I do have something to thank Mother for after all," she said, letting out a giggle.

A shrill sound was heard. She walked to the nightstand and picked up the phone. "Hello," she said. "Sonya Goldstein here."

"Good morning, Sonya. It's Jerry Fisher. I'm sorry to call you so early, but I promised to let you know the minute I found a gig, didn't I?"

"Oh yes! You sure did. Wow! Do you have something for me already? It's only been two days."

"Well, I don't know for sure. I can't promise anything. Won't know till they see you dance. Are you interested in letting them see you dance, Sonya?"

"Oh, you bet I am!"

"Great! Told you I'd come through for ya. Listen, one thing. Can you be in my office by nine o'clock?"

"But ... that's less than forty-five minutes from now," she said, her eyes darting around the room.

"I know. Sorry for being last minute. Think you can make it?"

"Of course, of course," she said, scanning her two dresses hanging on the rack. One was vibrant blue and the other jet-black. "I'll be there," she said. "Nine o'clock sharp."

"Good girl! That's what I wanted to hear. See ya then. And don't forget to bring your dancing shoes," he added, chuckling as he hung up.

She walked over to the clothes rack.

"Oh, I knew Aunt Sarah wouldn't let me down," she said, slipping the blue dress over her head. "She told me her friend would find work for me on Broadway. I knew I could count on her. Oooh, it's happening ... it's really happening!"

Checking her image in the mirror, Sonya smoothed out her skirt. "Great color," she said. "Makes my eyes sparkle." She finished combing her hair and was straightening the seam of her nylons when the phone rang again. "Must be Jerry with more details," she said, gliding across the room. "Okay, okay ... hold on, Jerry. I'm coming."

Sonya reached for the receiver. "Hi, Jerry," she said, grinning a little. "What did you forget to tell me?"

But it wasn't Jerry. It was her older brother.

"Forget to tell you? I didn't forget to tell you anything! And who the hell is Jerry? Listen, little sister, I'm in the office of the rundown dump you're in. I'm gonna give you just five minutes to get your bags packed. You'd better be ready to leave when I get there. Am I making myself clear?"

"But, Lenny—"

"But nothing, Sonya. I'm warning you. I've driven all night and I'm not very happy. What the hell were you thinking ... taking a bus from Cleveland to New York all by yourself?" He took a quick breath. "And when Mom gets her hands on Aunt Sarah, there's gonna be hell to pay."

Sonya was speechless. She bit her lip. "But Lenny ... this is my big chance. I'm gonna dance for someone in just—"

"Dance for someone? Are you crazy?"

"It's an audition, Lenny ... a real audition. I'll drive home with you right after, I promise."

"Have you lost your mind? Mom will kill me if I let you go through with that. You know how she feels about New York City. She sure doesn't think it's any place for a nineteen year old girl, I can tell ya that."

Tuning out her brother's ramblings, Sonya continued to plead. "Please Lenny. I promise to go with you right after. I prom—"

There was a click on the other end. The line went quiet.

Sonya toppled backwards on the bed. The phone dropped to the floor. "Why did Aunt Sarah have to tell? Darn it! She promised. She promised."

Then it happened.

Sonya didn't know when it first appeared in her life. But it had been with her as long as she could remember, showing up whenever anyone tried to hold her back from what she wanted. A smile filled her face. Her heart skipped a beat. In that instant, Sonya's eyes opened wide. She got up and started pacing the floor. On her third trip across the room and back, her voice nearly exploded.

"Ain't nobody gonna stop me from getting what I want. Not Lenny. Not Momma. Nobody!"

A loud knock was heard at the door.

"Coming Lenny," Sonya called out.

As she passed the dresser, Sonya picked up a slip of paper with Jerry's phone number. Carefully, she tucked it inside her bra.

"Another time, Jerry," she said. "Another time."

CHAPTER 20

None of us kids ever died on The Farm but we did have a few close calls.

Only one creek on our property was suitable for swimming. We simply called it The Creek. To get there, we followed a dirt path, and passed up a large shed. It was then just a short jaunt to a pasture surrounded by barbed wire fencing. Some days the power was turned on and other days it wasn't. To avoid any potential zap, we'd scoot underneath on our bellies. When the "juice" was flowing and we failed to get low enough, the shock felt like being kicked in the behind. Hard.

After clearing the fence, we walked across the cow-pie covered, weed-filled terrain toward the old oak tree. Then we strolled down the hill, dropped our towels on the dock, and plunged into the cold water. We had to move quickly to avoid the black, yucky bloodsuckers waiting to leech a meal off one of us kids. Needless to say, we couldn't swim fast enough past the mucky bottom and get to the stone-covered area nearby.

Kerri and I had lots of fun in those bloodsucker-infested waters. One summer we made up a synchronized dance routine. Our amazing performance went something like this: First, we pranced around in a circle, singing the lyrics to Jo Stafford's hit song, "Thank You for Calling."

We always sang the last line of the song after springing high into the air just before our big, splashy backwards flip finale. Minutes later, we'd be bobbing back up for another round.

Without adult supervision, the deep end of The Creek wasn't always the safest place to play. Especially for the Three Babies (Darla, Joey, and me) being watched by Big Kids, only a few years older.

On one sweltering afternoon, I begged Kerri to tow me into the cooler, deeper waters. She extended her crossed arms and I grabbed on. I flutter-kicked my way through the deep end; then climbed onto shore. We repeated this many times without incident. However, when Darla tried the same trick she wasn't nearly as brave.

Soon after Kerri towed Hal's six-year-old beyond the shallow water, her arms began thrashing around. Without warning, Darla grabbed onto Kerri's neck as if she'd discovered a floatation device with her name on it. Seconds later, they both went under ... a couple of times. Finally, Kerri managed to keep her head above water long enough to scream for help.

Todd, playing nearby, jumped in and quickly loosened Darla's "Oh my God, I'm drowning" grip from around Kerri's neck. Then he towed Darla safely to shore.

Without warning, Hal and Carter appeared on top of the hill. Unbeknown to us, they were repairing the fence surrounding the pasture.

"What's going on down there?" Hal called out.

"Nothing," Kerri hollered as casually as she could.

"I heard a call for help!" Hal hollered back.

"It's okay!" Todd yelled. "We're having fun, that's all."

"Well, don't call for help unless you need it!" he barked.

Kerri HAD needed help. But she didn't dare let Hal know that his "little princess" had been dangerously close to going under for the third time.

***

Hal seemed to love lavishing special gifts upon his children. At five, Darla squealed when he gave her Shauna, a two-foot tall doll with beautiful red hair. That doll's hair wasn't only beautiful; it was real. And it cascaded down to the center of her back.

At sixteen, Elizabeth was given a slightly beat-up Oldsmobile.

Carter's special gift was a chocolate-brown pony with snow-white spots on her body and head. Carter named her Snowball. A week or so after she arrived, our circular driveway was turned into a horseback-riding arena.

Darla and I didn't do any actual riding that day. Hal instructed Carter to put us in the saddle, hold onto the reins, and lead his pony around our driveway. Not a dangerous activity, I'll admit. Yet, that was how I almost lost my head ... literally.

It was all great fun until Carter momentarily let go of the reins.

Snowball probably took that as an indication our playtime was over. She saw the barn and headed for it ... with me on her back.

Several Big Kids started making a ruckus, but it was Todd's voice I heard above the rest.

"Nita ... pull on the reins!" my brother yelled. "Stop her! She's heading for the barn!"

When Snowball approached the barn door, another kid shouted, "Lay back! The beam! Watch out for the beam!"

Too petrified to follow directions, I had no choice but to let Snowball continue on her path. As the two-by-four, above the barn door, grazed my neck, Todd was by my side.

He grabbed my waist and yanked hard.

The two of us fell backwards onto the hot asphalt.

Snowball, apparently oblivious of my near decapitation, kept moving forward. I watched as she casually sauntered into her stall.

After that experience, I wondered if Carter would allow me to ride his pony again. If he did, I knew what I'd do. After I saddled her up, I'd head for the grassy area beside the road. Then I'd smack her on the backside and away we'd fly ... away from The Farm, away from Hal, away, away ...

I dreamed of traveling all the way to California where I'd contact Doris Day, my very favorite movie star. I always admired her positive nature, the way her eyes sparkled bright, and how everything worked out for her in the movies. I was sure she'd welcome me with open arms. Then my remaining years would be spent Doris Day style; a.k.a. happily-ever-after.

***

Hal didn't believe in doctors. He preached that sickness was all in the head. Therefore, if any adults got sick, they were at fault. Also, very little comfort or assistance was offered to a sick child. At age eight or nine, I remember cleaning up my vomit in the upstairs hall. My mother, of course, wasn't home. The only help extended was Edith's less than comforting words: "Darla got sick too, but at least *she* made it to the bathroom."

Hal believed that if any of the children got sick, it was their mother's fault. Here are two examples of his great wisdom:

Sonya's oldest child, Dennis, had a skin disorder on his leg. It caused a great deal of itching and inflammation. Hal informed Sonya the condition occurred because she was a bad mother.

Like many children, Gina had a habit of sucking her thumb.

"Your daughter wouldn't be sucking her thumb," he told Mom, "if you were a better mother."

I have no idea how my mother managed to get special permission for me when (at age eight) a doctor was needed to pump my stomach. But I'm sure grateful she did.

As our summer came to an end, the canning of fruits and vegetables took place on our extra stove in the basement. The kids did the picking, washing, and cutting. The grown-ups handled heating things up to proper temperatures and all the rest.

The day my stomach got pumped was a hot August afternoon.

The farmwomen were busy canning.

After playing outside for a short time, my throat got dry. I used the cellar entrance to escape the hot summer sun. The coolness of the basement offered some relief, but it was water I needed.

One of the kids pointed to a glass filled to the brim and asked if I was thirsty.

I nodded.

The kid pushed the liquid toward me.

"Looks good, doesn't it?" I heard.

I lifted the glass to my lips.

As the clear liquid found the back of my throat, I heard, "No! No, don't drink it. I was kidding."

Too late!

Mom saw my eyes roll to the back of my head. Then down I went ... onto the basement floor. It's no wonder! The fluid I swallowed wasn't meant for human consumption. It was a sealant used in the canning process. Mom called it "water glass."

CHAPTER 21

Most of the time, I didn't share private thoughts with anyone.

But with Joey (Sonya and Charlie's youngest son) things were different. Our special friendship began with digging in the sandbox and playing pretend. Later those activities morphed into hearty games of Canasta, Monopoly, and Clue.

After Charlie's family was banned from the Big House, Joey and I had to play outside, in the chicken coop, barn, or shed.

One day, Joey tried to challenge Hal's restriction by strolling through our back door as if everything were fine. That tactic didn't work for long. Not under Edith's watchful eye. She seemed to take great pleasure in escorting her nephew outside like he had the plague.

Soon I caught up to him.

We spent the first part of that afternoon in the barn, jumping off the high beam into the soft hay below. After awhile, Joey wanted to crawl through a tunnel the Big Kids had forged on the far side of the barn. To enter, we needed to scrunch down like soldiers. Then we crawled on our bellies boot camp style.

Joey approached the dank hay first.

I followed, inching along close behind. A strong, musty smell filled my nostrils. After a few twists and bends, I was pretty sure I'd made a wrong turn into a dungeon.

"Hey, Joey!" I yelled. "This is as far as I go. I'm turning back."

"Aw, don't be such a baby ... keep going," I heard him say from a place sounding miles away. "Come on. I'm at the window. There's plenty of light. You'll see. Keep going."

Finally there, I found Joey propped on his knees with a "what took ya so long" expression on his face.

We chatted, staring out the window, happy to be away from listening ears. We probably would have stayed longer except that I hadn't had my daily dose of candy yet.

I asked Joey if he wanted some.

"Sure," he replied, "but where do ya get candy?"

"From Hal," I said with a chuckle. "He's got a million boxes of the stuff lining his dresser in the library. He'll never miss a couple of chocolate creams."

Joey grinned. "What! Are you kidding? Do you really steal from Hal?"

"Yep!" I said, sounding quite proud of myself.

"Ever get caught?"

"Sort of," I said. "A month or so ago. Darla was napping there."

"What happened?"

"Well ... just as I was leaving with a pocketful, her head popped up from under the covers."

Joey laughed. "Did she mention it to you later?"

"All she said was she knew a secret about me. But when I questioned her further, she had nothing to say." I paused. "So ..." I said, looking at him coyly, "How many ya want?"

The remainder of that afternoon was spent enjoying sweet treats, courtesy of Hal, and we thought that it was mighty nice of him.

***

I'm sure our time together was more important to me than to Joey. He rarely complained about our lifestyle. No wonder. He lived in the Steel House away from our day-to-day traumas. Plus, he didn't hold a grudge against Darla. But I did.

Even as a young child, Hal's *little angel* showed a tendency toward high intelligence and artistic talents.

Naturally, I always felt like I couldn't measure up. Which was true, even for things I could effortlessly accomplish; like preparing a bowl of strawberries and sour cream for my father. It was easy to make. There really was nothing to it. I picked a bowl of strawberries; then stirred in a heaping tablespoon of sour cream.

My father made a big fuss, raving about how he loved the dessert, and how he'd never tasted anything quite so delicious.

Then Darla showed up with another bowlful.

When she asked which he liked best, my father took the low road and said, "I like them both the same."

Groan.

Also, it wasn't much fun watching Darla receive special gifts, like her doll with the real hair that I didn't dare touch. I'll tell you this much; it sure wasn't easy being green.

Green with envy, that is.

But that's where Joey came in. He was younger than me ... by a year and a half. However, any difference in our age was lost on me. Joey was a great sounding board, and he listened to the dreams I dared to dream.

We would spend entire afternoons under the apple tree on the School House lawn. As we gazed up at the clouds, we'd scope out bunnies and tigers as they floated by. Other times, we'd guess the destinations of airplanes overhead. I loved the idea of being whisked away on a wing of one of those planes. I believed if I could get up high enough, freedom would be just a few miles away.

My madcap plan involved grabbing a ladder from the barn and placing it atop our tallest evergreen. I'd add rungs until one of the wings was within reaching distance.

For Joey, a more realistic scheme involved digging a path to China. I wasn't opposed to giving that a whirl as well. We spent countless hours breaking up the ground with our sand box shovels. There were days when we went home covered in dirt. Still, it was "country" dirt (the grown-up's description), so it couldn't possibly hurt us (their theory). And I suppose that made sense. They grew up in city dwellings with no room to run and play, let alone get dirty.

Mom often said that we were the luckiest kids on earth. After all, we had acres of playground and never lacked playmates. I didn't agree with that viewpoint, and certainly didn't think we were lucky. But I did enjoy playing with Joey. He was a lot of fun; and cute, too.

He had sandy blond hair that he'd unconsciously twirl around his index finger, especially when tired.

Another thing, schoolwork was easy for Joey. He proved it by maintaining straight A's on his report card. For that accomplishment, his mom rewarded him with half a gallon of ice cream—any flavor he wanted.

Lucky Joey. As far as I could tell, he had three distinct advantages.

First, he lived in the Steel House, away from Hal's rules. I thought the only kid luckier than Joey was his kid brother, Matt. He was born seven years after Joey. By then, his family had been banned from the Big House and lived like a normal family.

Second, Joey had a mother who seemed interested in what he was doing.

And third, Joey enjoyed reading. That fact, coupled with Joey's willingness to help me, worked to my benefit in sixth grade. Well, almost.

I didn't really want to cheat in school. But what's a girl to do when her teacher assigns book reports every few months? Rewriting the back cover synopsis was one option, but not nearly as easy as asking Joey to write the whole thing. Recopying his notes was a snap. What a guy!

My sister, Kerri, didn't have such problems. She was an obsessive reader. "Books transport you into a different world," she'd often say.

That sounded appealing. Except that it didn't work for me. I couldn't remember from one paragraph to the next what I'd read.

I was convinced that asking Joey to write my report was a foolproof plan until my teacher announced in front of the class, "So, Anita, how long have you been interested in Gatling guns?"

***

The time came when my friendship with Joey was tested. It happened during the middle of summer when I was eight and a half and Joey seven. The Big Kids were playing baseball. Joey and I watched the game from the top of two slides. I sat on the tallest one; he was on the smaller replica.

Everything went well until Joey wanted to slide down the big slide. But that was where I was sitting. Thinking he planned to steal my prime viewing spot, I refused his request.

At first, the Big Kids ignored the clamor. But when our disagreement escalated, they decided to pick sides.

None of them chose mine.

Todd plopped down behind me and started shoving. Several others added their body weight. Who could win against such odds? But that didn't stop me. My palms burned from friction as, inch by inch, they shoved me down the slide. When I reached the bottom, I realized that I'd wet my pants.

Crying all the way home, I was relieved to see Gina in my parents' bedroom. I rushed to her for comfort. That was my next mistake.

"I saw the whole thing from the window," she said sternly. "You should have let Joey have that slide."

My sister was right, of course. But at the time, her reaction felt like one more shove down that slide.

CHAPTER 22

We did have some fun on The Farm. But it was a means of survival. Early in our lives we discovered humor to be our best defense. We also learned one or two avenues of escape.

For me, it was pretending to be someone famous in front of Mom's full-length mirror.

Kerri loved getting lost in a good book. Reading was her favorite pastime. Going for walks was a close second. And when her travels included a trip through the woods, Todd and I often tagged along.

One afternoon, our exploring stopped when a swarm of wasps started buzzing above Kerri's head.

"Get 'em off me! Get 'em off me!" she screamed at Todd.

But he only laughed at her dilemma.

A few days later, Kerri was ready for another trek through the woods.

"Where's Ginger?" Kerri asked. "It's more fun when she's with us."

We found our lovable pet stretched out under the lilac bush with Casey.

When Ginger saw us, her tail wagged like a windshield wiper gone wild.

"Ya know what I love about Ginger?" Kerri said in a teasing voice.

I'd heard that question dozens of times. I played along anyway.

"What?" I asked.

"Her tail wags when she's happy."

I giggled. "Then she must be happy all the time."

"She is," Kerri said. "Look at her. You ready, girl?"

Ginger's ears tilted and her eyes seemed to say: *Sure. What's up? What's next?*

"Yeah ... you're ready," Kerri said. "C'mon. Let's go."

Todd was wearing his favorite shirt. Images of cowboys lassoing cattle were on the collar, sleeves, and everywhere else. He called it his rodeo shirt. Before we left, he completed his outfit by flinging his trusty bow and arrow over his shoulder. It was a toy set that he'd gotten for Christmas. He liked having it handy. "In case we see wild animals," he'd say.

We headed down the path toward Snail Woods.

Ginger walked between us, her little feet scampering along.

We went deep into the woods that day, where the trees were thick, and the temperature muggy. For a while, we cooled ourselves off by swinging on monkey vines. Then Kerri suggested we'd be a lot cooler if we waded in The Lagoon.

"We gotta be careful though," she said, using her grown-up voice. "Don't forget ... that's where the wasps got me before."

"I can shoot that thing down from here," Todd said, when he spotted the nest. Then he grabbed an arrow from his pack and placed it across the string.

"No, Todd. You shouldn't do that!" Kerri hollered.

Ignoring all warning, our brother pulled back his bow. "Those wasps won't dare pester us again," he said.

"No! You'd better not!" Kerri shrieked.

All of a sudden, a bunch of scary-looking, black-and-yellow pests were ready for battle.

While they swarmed Todd's head and he danced around trying to get away from them, it was his turn to scream, "Get 'em off me! Get 'em off me!"

It was also Kerri's turn to laugh.

"Guess he doesn't think it's so darn funny now, does he?" Kerri said, watching Todd charge toward The Lagoon, a parade of wasps in hot pursuit.

CHAPTER 23

The school year at Cheltenham Elementary began with the clanging of cymbals followed by a musical procession to a nearby community church. The more talented students were given the triangles. Not me. I usually got stuck with the sticks. That instrument was nothing more than two pencil-like pieces of wood that, when struck together, created some sort of non-musical tone.

Even though I wasn't musically inclined, some of the Big Kids were. By far, the most talented was Charlie's oldest son, Dennis. At one time, Charlie had earned a living playing in a band. He was extremely passionate about his music and became completely disheartened when he had to quit to find a better source of income. He put his trumpet down and never played it again.

Dennis must have inherited his father's talents. He started out as First Trumpet in his high school's marching band. Then he went on to become a top-level, prize-winning trumpet player. His natural ability awarded him a scholarship to the Cleveland Institute of Music. Also, he studied at the Hruby Conservatory of Music in Cleveland. Later, he was elected into his high school's Alumni Hall of Fame. However, before all that happened, Dennis had the honor of meeting one of the most famous trumpet players of all time: Louis Armstrong.

When Dennis was thirteen, Charlie was scheduled to take pictures of that well-known performer. He treated his son to the show. During intermission, a photo was snapped in the star's dressing room. (See photo insert.)

Another time, Louis Armstrong came to the studio for promotional pictures. At that time, the Jazz Great taught Dennis a few of his special techniques.

All of the grown-ups loved jazz and often frequented the clubs throughout Cleveland, New York City, and elsewhere. Armed with photographs that Charlie (or others from The Studio) had previously taken, Hal would stroll into the clubs with a camera bag draped over his shoulder. Then, during breaks in the show, he'd display those photos in front of the performers.

He'd always bring along Charlie, Mom, Dad, or others who worked at The Studio. Although they considered it a treat to see the celebrities, their attendance was a necessity. Hal was not a photographer. He needed to have someone else take the pictures.

One camera produced stereo slides. Once developed, there would be two images per slide. Viewers would place the slide into a hand-held box with a built-in light. What they'd see would be a spectacular color image in 3-D. The color was vibrant and the pictures life-like.

Hal would set the box in front of the Jazz Greats and say, "Look at the picture I took of you."

Seeing photographs taken in magnificent color (when all others were in black and white) wowed the performers. The pictures snapped on one night became Hal's entry to the next group of musicians. His "silver tongue" gave him further access to the stars. Not all of the performers had made it "big" yet. They appreciated the special attention as well as seeing the impressive photos.

Often the Cleveland Jazz Club held post-jam session parties at The Studio. After the session, Hal would brag about our "utopian" lifestyle. Several artists (Earl "Fatha"

Hines, Barney Bigard, and Darnell Howard) even came to The Farm for a visit. Maxine Sullivan stayed with us for several days. During her visit, she played her popular rendition of "Loch Lomond" on the piano in our living room.

Another time, Hal befriended a local performer who visited us on multiple occasions. He even posed for a picture with Hal's daughter, Darla, on his shoulders; piggyback style. At the time, very few people were aware of this young man's talent. It was, however, only a matter of time before everyone across the country knew the name Frankie Laine.

Hal, braggart that he was, insisted he was the one who purchased Frankie Laine's first suit prior to the singer heading out West to make it big. Who knew if that story was true? Not me. I loved his songs though, and got teary-eyed with emotion whenever his hit tune "I Believe" played on the radio. Those beautiful lyrics were my introduction to a true higher power.

CHAPTER 24

During the summer before my third school year, most families on The Farm decided that denying true feelings, while playing the role of enthusiastic followers, had lost its appeal. Gathering up their children, they bid farewell to The Farm. Then they headed down the road they must have previously only dreamed of traveling—the one leading away from Hal.

As a result of their departure, most of our farming stopped. We continued to grow a huge garden, but with limited farmhands, all animals (except for the dogs, a few dozen rabbits, and Carter's pony) were sold.

The only remaining inhabitants in the Big House were Hal, Edith, their children, and my family. Wait. That's not completely accurate. We always found room for the children belonging to the Sunday Regulars—a group of city folks (mostly women) who strongly believed in Hal, but never moved to The Farm. They would drive the forty plus miles nearly every Sunday for a visit. Sometimes they'd drop off their children for a summer, or school year or two. I refer to their kids as Children For a Season.

Joey's family still lived in the Steel House.

The School House was home for Teresa, an exotic, dark-haired beauty and youngest of the farmwomen. She shared the house with her husband, Bill, and their two children. Their son, Johnny, was my brother's age. They also had an adorable baby girl, named Lynette. She was sweet and cuddly; with small wisps of blonde curls hugging the nape of her neck. Even though Lynette was technically a baby, she didn't qualify to become a fourth edition to the "Three Babies" clan. That group never extended beyond Joey, Darla and me.

Although I was only seven and a half that summer, Teresa must have considered me responsible. She often asked me to keep a watchful eye on her toddler.

One time, cute little Lynette giggled while I pushed her on the swings. But when I took my turn ... BAM! She got whacked and fell to the ground. Fortunately, Hal bypassed his negative feelings concerning doctors. Or perhaps it was Teresa who insisted that her daughter's arm be examined. I have no idea. All I know for certain is the next time I saw Lynette, her arm was in a sling.

Another time, a few of us kids were testing to see how far we could push bobby pins into electrical outlets before getting zapped. Just a normal day of fun, right? What harm could there be?

Unfortunately, Lynette found out.

By days end, she resembled a pint-sized Joe Palooka heading for the ring. Enormous bandages covered both of her fists.

A few weeks later, Lynette and her family also moved away. I hope her mother found a more conscientious baby-sitter, or at least one past the age of seven.

CHAPTER 25

Before that summer ended, Joey, Darla, and I formed a club intended strictly for us. So naturally, when we held private gatherings in Casey's doghouse, we had to post a NO BIG KIDS ALLOWED sign.

Not much went on during our meetings. We'd bring peanut butter and jelly sandwiches and play a few games. One afternoon, Joey's brother, Greg, decided to invade our territory.

We got mad and yelled, "Can't ya read? No Big Kids Allowed!"

Then we hooked the latch on the door to let him know that we meant business. Our exuberance faded with the sound of a bolt turning on the outside. Oh no! Now *we* were locked in.

Still, that wasn't much of a problem. Not for the Three Babies. We could easily scurry through the doggie door. Then all we had to do was climb over Casey's fence. Our plan couldn't fail.

First up was Darla. She easily maneuvered her body through the small opening, effortlessly cleared the fence, and then dropped to the ground. So did Joey. When my turn came, up and over I went. Up ... up ... and over.

Missed it by that much.

My index finger didn't quite make the leap. Howling in pain, my skin clung to the barbed wire as if it were part of our plan.

Joey ran for help.

That time it was Dodgy-Daddy to the rescue.

I was a toddler when I began calling my father that name. Story has it that I had a difficult time saying the word "Daddy." Instead, it came out "Dodgy."

At any rate, he was working in a nearby pasture and came running.

With one quick, sharp yank, I was free to play another day.

Dodgy-Daddy, or "Dodge," as I liked to call him, was a quiet, gentle man. He also had big, bulging muscles. On Sunday mornings when I'd wake him, he'd make a big

144

production out of stretching. First, he'd raise his arms high in the air. Then he'd arch his back and slowly ease his upper body into a big, sleepy stretch. That's when his muscles popped way out.

Sunday afternoons were usually good for a round or two of hangman with Dodge. That game was an "old school" version of *Wheel of Fortune*. While waiting for supper, I'd sit on his lap, trying to guess letters to his selected words.

Trouble was, that darned dinner bell always rang too soon.

CHAPTER 26

When I entered third grade, Pam and Nancy were still in a different classroom. I shared space with second graders.

Mom continued to work at The Studio. I missed her something awful and kept hoping that things would change. Her absence became almost unbearable when Edith came to tuck Darla in at night. She must have thought I took up too much space in the bunk I shared with her daughter. She was constantly shoving me over to give Darla more room. I'd lie awake with my eyes shut tight, wishing they'd stop talking and giggling. That's when I missed Mom the most.

Gina and Todd were tall for their age. I was average, and Kerri was probably the shortest in her class. But she had a big loving heart, angelic face, and sweet disposition. On top of that, she had beautiful jet-black hair. The older she got, the more her positive traits emerged.

Hal showered Kerri with adoration. Soon he elevated her into the same category as his own children. Taking all cues from their leader, the grown-ups joined him in treating Kerri like the Golden Girl of Erehwon.

At one time, Hal even moved Kerri into the School House. His family was sleeping there at the time. Finally, Kerri asked. "Please, Mom … can't I please come back to the Big House with you?"

Naturally, Mom had to ask Hal about that.

In the end, Hal did allow Kerri to return, but never stopped lavishing privilege upon her, even treating her to Billie Holiday's performance at the Sky Bar in Cleveland. He went on behalf of The Studio to schmooze with the jazz artists. That job came naturally for him. Building people up was his specialty. Sadly, so was tearing them down.

Kerri found that out in seventh grade. I was in third, Todd in fifth, and Gina was a freshman in high school.

That winter, heavy snowfalls kept us housebound for days. So, when Hal invited Kerri, Todd, Carter, and me to the movies, we were thrilled.

Hal parked his 1951 silver Lincoln about two blocks from the theater.

Driving such an impressive car was almost unheard of in our town. But nothing was too good for Hal. His vehicle came equipped with windows that opened and closed with the push of a button.

I suppose Hal believed he deserved luxury transportation while we wore hand-me-downs. Besides, didn't he need to impress the jazz artists when he drove them to The Farm?

We walked the snow-covered sidewalks to the only entertainment spot in town. Hal purchased tickets. Then, as lights began to flicker, he led us down the center aisle.

"Grab those seats," he told Todd and me.

Carter sat down in front of my brother. Hal sat in front of me, and Kerri scooted into the seat on the other side of him.

Todd and I were looking for a place for our jackets when Hal said, "Here ... give me those." He reached out with both hands.

Todd was eager to oblige. I wasn't. Usually, I got cold midway through a movie. "I'll keep mine," I said.

"No, you won't," Hal shot back. "Your sister's cold."

I didn't know how Kerri could possibly be cold with several jackets already covering her. But what choice did I have? I handed mine over, too.

"Enjoy the show," Hal said, adding his coat to the heap.

When the movie ended, and credits started to roll, Hal returned our jackets. Then he left to get the car.

Waiting on the curb with the others, the expression on Kerri's face told me that something was horribly wrong.

The next day Edith informed us that Kerri deserved the silent treatment. "After all," she said, Kerri is refusing to talk to Hal."

It seemed that Edith viewed the situation like this: If Hal was willing to give Kerri the privilege of listening to her, and she refused to talk to him, then she deserved to be shunned. That appeared to be the opinion of all the grown-ups—including Mom and Dad.

I didn't listen to such nonsense. Kerri was the only one who spent any time with me. She offered help with homework, and did things for me that Mom should have been doing, but wasn't. She also read stories to me from the *Honey Bunch* series. As she read, she'd hug my neck and call me Sugar Bunch, insisting I was much sweeter than honey.

And now Edith was telling me not to talk to her? I knew that was crazy. I also knew that if she and the other grown-ups put 2 + 2 together they might come up with 324 (or some other insane number) as long as "Hal said so." That was the logic under which we lived. We knew better. Heck, anyone would know better. But all the adults would be united in their belief that 324 had to be the correct answer. And hell would be paid if we questioned it. So we lived in a state of bewilderment and kept quiet, all the while shaking our heads in confusion. Ours was a world where insanity ruled most of the time. A good portion of my childhood was spent trying to make sense of things that made absolutely no sense at all. Not talking to Kerri was just one of them.

When Saturday cleaning chores rolled around (which Kerri refused to do), Edith had the audacity to remind me about how bad my sister was.

"And after everything Hal's done for her!" she said in her most indignant tone.

I had no idea what she was talking about and would have thrown my mop in her face if I hadn't been such a coward.

The following week I noticed Kerri lying under the apple tree. She was flat on her back on the cold ground, gazing into space. Ever since that night at the theater Kerri spent most days by herself, or away from home.

"Whaddya doing?" I asked, stooping to her line of vision.

She didn't see me. Or if she did, I couldn't tell. She continued to stare out without expression.

"Kerri, what's going on?"

"Nothing," she said flatly.

"Then why do you look so strange?" I asked, waving my hand in front of her eyes to break the trance.

"No reason," she said. Then she got up and started to leave.

"Kerri! Wait up!" I called.

She turned and waited.

"What's with you?" I said. "I hardly see you anymore."

"That's 'cause nobody talks to me anymore," she said. "Mom, Dad, and everyone else. They all treat me like I've got leprosy."

"What do you mean?" I asked. "What's leprosy?"

"Never mind," she said. "I'm being shunned. So why should I hang around this place?"

"But why aren't we supposed to talk to you? It doesn't make any sense."

"Nothing around this place makes sense," she said. "I used to believe Hal had all the answers. I thought he was wonderful. But now—"

Kerri struggled to find words to explain; then stopped trying. Her eyes filled with tears.

A few days later, Kerri told me to check the blackboard in our basement. I was shocked to see what she'd written.

Across the middle were the words GO TO HELL.

"It's for all the grown-ups who are shunning me," she said.

I admired her courage, but was afraid for her.

"We'd better erase it," I said with concern. "You'll just get into more trouble."

It was an unusual thing for Kerri to do and completely out of character. However, she didn't act one bit worried about any possible consequence.

"What else can they do to me?" she said. "Leave it!"

From Singer's *Cults in Our Midst* (265):

"Many children reared in cults are truly victims who are especially alone and without advocates."

153

CHAPTER 27

Our chicken coop had multiple uses. None of them had anything to do with chickens. Hundreds of rabbits had taken over their cages years before. That didn't change the building's name.

There were several rooms on the second floor. One held musical instruments, including a set of drums and a brand new xylophone. No one ever played them. Another room had about a hundred rolls of wallpaper that never found their way onto a wall. Are we beginning to sense a pattern here, people?

Most undertakings were left unfinished, and numerous things never got used. Like the pile of lumber stacked behind the School House for years.

"It's only temporary," Hal would state at the onset of each new venture. It seemed to me that those words gave him license for indefinite procrastination.

Still, tasks like pouring cement to replace the wooden path leading to our front door never made it past the thinking stage. Only temporary, my behind! That walkway was never more than weatherworn boards plopped together with weeds growing in between.

Then there was Hal's dream of transforming The Lagoon into a resort. That grandiose scheme turned a shallow body of water into an overgrown swamp.

Also, let's not forget Hal's plans to add a garage onto the Big House. The cement was poured, and brick walls were constructed on each side. At that point, all work came to a halt. Hey, who needs a roof over a garage, right?

I have to admit that some of Hal's ideas did come to fruition. Like turning the second floor of the chicken coop into a theater. Hal had access to old movies and sometimes, on a Sunday, he'd set up a screen and projector to show silent films.

In one movie, Charlie Chaplin was struggling to carry an enormous safe down a staircase. Heaven only knows where Hal found that little gem. But who asked questions?

Also, Hal owned what was probably one of the first musical videos ever made. In it, the Mills Brothers sat cutting out paper dolls while singing their hit song of that title, "Paper Doll."

We had our own creative films as well. They were a hoot. Who'd think watching people walk in fast motion (which was the way home movies once looked) could be so comical?

My favorite one featured Kerri and me when Lynette was learning to walk. As the movie began, Kerri was seen crouching beside the eleven-month-old. Then the unsuspecting child was turned loose to gleefully toddle toward my outstretched arms.

I couldn't seem to understand the concept of our movie camera. And so, despite countless explanations, my eyes stayed glued to the camera. Consequently, each time Charlie filmed the action, Lynette went toddling completely off course. You'd think after awhile I'd catch a clue. I guess grasping things quickly wasn't my specialty. Apparently, causing toddlers to fall to the ground was.

Even though movie night was great fun, I'd usually get tired before the last reel of film was played. One time, after I fell asleep, Dad carried me back to the house. I didn't stir until the squeak of our front door startled me.

Where was I?

A few seconds later, I knew. I was in my daddy's arms. How I cherished that moment ... being held.

CHAPTER 28

I *always believed that my father was the strongest man alive. Yet, at the same time, he was weak ... unable to leave The Farm. That contradiction confused me. While it didn't answer all my questions, somewhere in my fifties, Dad shared this story with me:*

NICK'S STORY – AGE ELEVEN

Nick watched his mother carefully place her last piece of china into an old cardboard box.

"Don't forget to bring home the Italian bread tonight," she said. "And listen, Nick, don't let him give you any of that stale stuff. It needs to last us a couple of days. And get two loaves. Don't forget now." She took a quick breath. "Oh ... and Nick, be sure to come home right after work ... right after he pays you. You *will* be getting paid tonight, won't you?"

"Yeah, Ma. Sure. I'll get paid. And I won't forget the bread ... two loaves ... the freshest he's got." Nick gave his mother a quick smile. "I'll get the money, pick up the bread, and then come right home. I promise."

Nick's house was small and the furnishings were not fancy. Now, almost everything they owned was stacked in the living room. In the morning, a moving truck would be parked in their driveway. By afternoon, his whole family would be boarding a train for Pittsburgh.

At least that's what Nick's mother had been saying for the past week. And with boxes piling higher every day, Nick had no reason to doubt her. Besides, once his mother made up her mind, no one could change it. She always had the final word.

Things were different in his Uncle Gino's house. If Uncle Gino and Aunt Victoria were moving, his uncle would be the one making plans.

Nick's favorite uncle was tall and powerfully built. While Gino was a boisterous Italian man, Nick's dad was quiet. He allowed his wife to make all the decisions. So, when she flatly announced that they were moving, Nick and his brothers—one older and two younger—knew better than to protest.

Nick's parents had arrived on Ellis Island (from Italy) when their firstborn was a year old. Two years later, Nick became their first child born in America. In time, two more boys brought the family total to six.

All his life, Nick had lived in the same neighborhood. His home was located in a "Little Italy" setting with other immigrants and their families.

Now, at eleven years old, everything was changing. In Pittsburgh he wouldn't know anyone or have any friends.

Nick worked two jobs for over a year. One was at his father's grocery store, the other at Mr. Giovanetti's bakery. He especially liked working at the bakery. Mr. Giovanetti paid him. Not much, but enough to put aside a few coins each week before giving the rest to his mother.

Still, those coins added up. Eventually, Nick had enough to buy a neighbor kid's bike. It wasn't exactly new. The tires kept going flat, and patches of rust threatened to cover over the original robin's-egg blue frame.

"It's time," his mother called from the doorway. "Hurry up. You're gonna be late!"

Over the next four hours Nick washed the bakery shelves and re-stocked them. He ran errands, listened to his boss complain about his wife, and tell stories about the kids. After sweeping the floor, Nick put away the broom and hung up his apron. Then he approached his boss.

"Good job today, Nick. Here's your money for the last two weeks. You earned it. You're a good worker, you know that, kid?" he said, pressing some coins and a few dollar bills into Nick's hand.

Nick gave him a warm smile. "Thank you Mr. Giovanetti."

"You're welcome. Now be a good boy and go over and pick out a nice loaf of bread for your mother." Grinning at Nick, he gestured toward the rack in back of the store.

"Ma needs two loaves. We have six in our family," Nick said. "Can I take two?"

"Sure, kid, sure." He chuckled a little. "Think of it as a going away gift. I'm sure gonna miss ya, kid, you know that?"

Instead of answering, Nick strolled over and selected two loaves from the front shelves. He sniffed them to check their freshness. He realized his boss expected him to take day-old bread, but that wasn't what his mother wanted.

"These okay?" Nick asked, holding them up for inspection.

His boss smiled. "Sure, kid. Don't worry about it. I like you, Nick. You're a good kid."

"Thanks Mr. Giovanetti. Sorry my family has to move. I hope we'll come back someday. If we do, I'll work for you again, okay?"

"Sure, kid, sure. Take care now."

Nick placed both loaves into the basket he'd wired to the front of his bike. He shoved the money into his pocket, jumped on his bike, and peddled home.

The next morning Nick woke up to a house filled with commotion. His father was helping two men—one they called Rocco and the other one Jake—drag their living room couch out the front door.

His mother was shouting orders at everyone.

By noon, all the furniture, boxes and everything they owned had been piled onto a big truck.

Well, everything, except for one item--Nick's bike. He was riding it through the neighborhood.

"You're gonna have to get off that thing sooner or later!" his mother hollered as he began what would have been his final trip around. "Everything goes. Now get back here!"

Her stern voice brought Nick to a screeching halt.

Then one of Rocco's big hands seized Nick from behind, toppling him off his bike.

Nick jumped up. "I'll pack it myself!" he said, eyeing a piece of rope lying on the ground. He tied his bike to the living room couch. Then he tugged on it, making sure it wouldn't fall over when Rocco rounded a corner too fast.

Rocco sauntered up to Nick's mother, his face dripping with perspiration. Wiping his brow with a handkerchief, he placed paperwork in front of her.

"Sign here ... and here," he said, pointing a sweaty finger in two places.

"Here's your money," she said, counting it out. Then she studied the papers, paying special attention to the box marked "Destination."

"Can you read our new address okay?" she asked, returning the papers.

"Sure can. 5185 North Pine Street, Pittsburgh, Pennsylvania. I can read it fine. Don't worry, ma'am. I'll make sure everything gets there okay. See ya in Pittsburgh," he said, waving goodbye. Then, over his shoulder, he told everyone to have a safe trip.

"Yeah ... you, too. See ya in Pittsburgh," she said.

At the door of his truck, Rocco turned to Nick. "That's where you'll find your bike, kid," he said with a wink.

Nick's eyes stayed fixed to the ground. His brothers had observed everything, but weren't saying a word. When Nick finally looked up, the truck had vanished out of sight.

His mother breathed in; then let out a heavy sigh. She turned to her husband. "Well, that's that. We did it! It's over."

He nodded. "Yes, it's over. Thank God!"

Nick's parents stared in the direction Rocco had driven. In a tone far from patient, his mother blurted out, "Where the hell's your brother? You told him to be here by noon, didn't you?"

"Don't worry. Gino will be here in time. You worry too much."

"Sure-sure. I worry too much. It's already going on one o'clock. That train leaves at three. Remember?"

"Gino knows we gotta catch that train. He'll be here!"

"Then *where* is he already? We gotta make that train. It's the only one going to Cleveland today."

"What?" Nick said. "Cleveland! What do you mean, Cleveland? You said we were moving to Pittsburgh."

"I know, Nick. But you don't understand. There were tough guys ... guys wanting money ... a lot of money. More money than we have."

"You need money?" Nick said frantically. "I can give you money. I've been saving up every week. You can have it all."

"Oh, Nick, you don't have that kind of money." She was annoyed and her voice showed it. "Nick, you don't understand! I'm talking about tough guys … guys wanting more and more money from the store."

Nick looked confused. "What store?"

"What store do you think?" his father yelled. "My grocery store. Every month they wanted more, more, more. Well, guess what? We don't have any more." He stopped talking; then turned toward his wife for help.

"Don't you understand, Nick," his mother added. "We *have* to get out. There's no other way."

"But, Ma, we'll never see our stuff again."

A split second later, Nick was screaming.

"My bike! My bike is on that truck!"

Exasperated, his mother heaved a heavy sigh.

"Hurry!" Nick said. "I'll bet if we hurry we can catch up with them. Wait. I know," he said. "Call Uncle Gino! Maybe Uncle Gino can catch them."

When all pleas were ignored, Nick lost control. "I want my bike back!" he screamed.

"Shaddup, Nick! Listen to me. I don't give a damn what you want. Do you hear me? I told you, we're never gonna see our stuff again, and that's that."

She drew in a slow breath and released it. "Now, I don't want to hear another word about it. Not one more word. We're safe now. That's *all* that matters."

"Safe?" Nick said. "Safe from what?"

His mother shot him a familiar look—the one indicating all patience was gone. "Can't you understand anything? Listen, those guys are gonna be hunting for us. You don't think they'll give up so easy, do you? No, those guys will be looking for us all right."

"Yeah," her husband cut in with a chuckle. "They'll be looking for us all over Pittsburgh. But all of us," he said, winking at his wife, "all of us will be in Cleveland."

"You're right!" she said, a wave of relief rising from deep within. "We did it. We fooled them."

Thinking about their clever plan made Nick's parents start to giggle. That's when his brothers joined in the merriment. Soon everyone was laughing uncontrollably. Everyone, that is, except Nick.

My father told me he wanted to share his feelings with his mother. He wanted to believe she'd care. But he knew it was hopeless. He knew she wouldn't listen. With every mile the train traveled, he could feel himself retreating further and further within.

CHAPTER 29

*P*erhaps the most difficult aspect of our lifestyle was not having any advocates. My parents were rarely home, and in their absence, no one took their place. It seemed like I didn't belong to anyone. *Didn't Mom and Dad care about me? Didn't they care how I felt ... about anything? The intensity of those feelings became amplified on days when everything went horribly wrong.*

Kerri burst into the Girls' Room. Her eyes were red and puffy. It was a Sunday, so Mom and Dad were home. Kerri was thirteen; I was nine.

"She's dead! She's dead!" Kerri shrieked, rushing over to me. "She's dead!" she yelled again in terror.

"Kerri! W-what is it?" I asked. "What's wrong?"

"Oh, Nita! It's Ginger!" She burst into tears. "She's dead. Ginger's dead!"

"No!" I gasped. "She can't be dead!"

Kerri rushed to the window above my bunk. "She's out there!" Kerri cried, pounding the glass with her fist. "With Dad. Dad's with her."

"Dad's with her?" A sense of relief rushed over me. "Then she's okay!"

"No. She's not okay," Kerri snapped. "She'll never be okay. Ginger ran into the road. A truck—"

"But Dad's with her," I cut in. "He'll help her. Dad can fix her."

"No!" Kerri said in an angry voice. "I'm trying to tell you ... Ginger's dead! She got hit by a truck."

The news got worse.

"Dad had to shoot her ... to put her out of her misery."

"No! No!" I screamed, not wanting to believe this was true.

"Mom wouldn't let me go to her. She told me that seeing her would only make things worse."

"Oh, No!" I screamed again, the full impact of this tragedy finally registering. It felt like my heart had been crushed and ripped from my chest. I loved Ginger. She couldn't be dead. I thought about the stories I'd made up about her, how I called her Ginger-Cake, and how very much I loved her.

The next day, Kerri and I still weren't willing to accept that our Ginger was truly gone. We went to the barn, hoping to find her. A wagon was there, an old pair of skates, and a rusty bike ... but no Ginger.

Still refusing to believe the truth, we walked back to the wooded area. Within the deepest part of our beings we hoped that our beloved pet might miraculously be alive.

At mid-morning we reached Snail Woods. We remembered how Ginger loved to explore the cave above the hill. Maybe she'd be nearby. To get there, we had to pass the Junk Pile. A cracked toilet lid sat next to a rusty sink. Broken chairs, faded and falling apart were tossed on top of our old wringer washer. When we had almost given up, to our shock and horror, we found Ginger.

That once beautiful collie was stretched out on top of the heap, her legs forever frozen in place, a bullet hole in her head.

Kerri and I couldn't believe what we saw. We couldn't accept that our Ginger had been tossed aside like trash. As if Kerri hadn't tended to her night and day when a pup ... as if I didn't make up stories about her ... as if we never loved her ...

CHAPTER 30

Fourth grade started out better than any previous school year.

For openers, after being separated from Pam and Nancy in second and third grades, the three of us were finally reunited. I thought things couldn't get any better. Then something even more amazing happened.

Although Hal believed Mom's quality time (spent with me once a week) was more important than being home every day, he informed Mom that she could take a day off work midweek. Oh boy, did I ever fly off the school bus on Wednesdays!

One of my favorite "quality time" sessions with Mom involved making breaded pork chops. I'd push a stool up to the stove and together we'd dip the chops in beaten eggs and seasoned breadcrumbs. Then we'd plop them into a hot frying pan and watch as they sizzled away. Other times, Mom spent hours helping me with spelling and multiplication tables. But outlining a geography chapter proved to be the most valuable use of our one-on-one time.

My fourth grade teacher, short and plump, had been a permanent fixture in that classroom since Columbus sailed the ocean blue.

At least, that's what I thought. Otherwise, why would she fire off so many questions about Magellan and those other adventure-seeking explorers? Once her assault got underway, I'd hunker down at my desk and pray for the recess bell to call a cease-fire.

However, after Mom taught me her secret formula for remembering facts (outlining chapters), I was transformed into the wiz-kid of fourth grade ... at least for one day. Whatever Mrs. Potts wanted to know, I had the answer. I proved it by frantically waving my hand in the air.

Nine or ten questions later, my teacher stopped everything. She closed her book, stared out at the class, and posed one final query:

"Isn't there anyone in this class, *besides* Anita, who read their geography assignment?"

Smile!

Still, things weren't perfect. Some genius in our school system decided to expand my classroom to include all third graders. Guess what that meant? Yep, I had one more school year with Darla. Which also meant the "comparison game" would continue at school as well as at home. That was one game I'd never win.

Mom reminded me of that when an arithmetic problem had me stumped. The thought-provoking equation went something like this: If Mary has ten oranges, and Linda takes away three, and her mother gives her one more, how many oranges will Mary have left?

Sure, it sounds easy now. However, in grade school, where concentration had no place in my life, such problem-solving skills were way too complex.

The next day was Mom's day off. Before the bus arrived, I asked for her help. And she tried. Really, she did. Yet, after exhaustive explanations, she became frustrated. With a wild burst of anger, Mom grabbed my homework and presented the problem to Darla. In less time than it took me to ponder the first segment, she was back with the answer.

"Thank you," my mother said, acting like Hal's *little genius* had mastered Einstein's theory of relativity.

Then she turned to me. "See," she said through clenched teeth, "even Darla knows how to do that problem. And she's a year younger than you."

I hoped my mother would calm down. I needed the answer to that problem, not a lecture. What I got was a smack across the face, followed by a few choice, all-too familiar, words:

"Why can't you be more like Darla?"

CHAPTER 31

On the day we celebrated my ninth birthday, Darla approached me with her shoebox filled with assorted paper dolls, their clothing, shoes, and accessories.

"Wanna play?" she asked.

"Sure," I said, retrieving my own box of cutouts from Mom's bottom drawer. After rummaging through the box a short while, I let out a shriek. My Betty Grable was missing. She had curly, golden hair, with legs posed in a confident stance. I had party clothes for her; a mink stole and fancy showgirl outfits. She was my absolute favorite paper doll. And she was gone.

"Where's my Betty Grable? I said, accusing Darla of the crime. "Where is she?"

"How should I know? I didn't take her," she said.

"You must have! I had her yesterday."

"Well, I didn't take her," Darla repeated. Then she stormed away.

Like a bolt of lightning, Mom was on the scene, igniting the place with her fury.

"For heaven's sake, Nita!" she said. "I took your precious paper doll. But here ... take it." She threw my prized possession at me. "Now you've ruined everything!" she said before stomping away.

I was completely baffled. *Now I'd ruined everything?* That didn't make sense.

At candle blowing out time, I was even more confused. On my three-layer birthday cake there was a poodle drawn with pink frosting next to the inscription, YOU ARE A DOG.

Many years later, I learned that my mother had originally planned to draw Betty Grable on my cake next to the words, YOU ARE A DOLL.

I feel certain that Hal made the final decision in that cake decorating switcheroo. After all, he instigated every choice the grown-ups ever made.

CHAPTER 32

When my class had been split up, in second and third grades, it was Pam I missed the most. Now, in fourth grade, her desk was directly across from mine.

She was as sweet and pretty as ever. Her honey-blond hair now fell in beautiful waves to her shoulders. I admired everything about Pam. First of all, everyone loved her. Secondly, her appearance was perfection-plus, without a stitch or hair out of place.

Nancy sat directly behind me. Her Shirley Temple ringlets looked more relaxed now, as if someone had poked them with a stick to set them free. Her dimples continued to mask her mean streak, but it was still there, waiting to spring forth. Nevertheless, Nancy and Pam were a team. And that was one team I wanted to be on.

Laura was also back where she belonged—with me. We played together in first grade, and now she sat in front of me. She was sweet and kind with white-blonde hair cropped to her chin. I liked Laura, yet couldn't understand why she preferred pasta without meat sauce at lunchtime and brought a bagged lunch on sloppy-Joe day. How could anyone not like that spicy concoction? Most kids agreed that it was the best thing on the menu. No wonder Laura was pencil-thin.

Still, Laura and I had a lot in common. For one thing, we both had poker-straight hair. That's how Mom described mine while she slathered on the smelly Toni Home Permanent solution, and struggled to coax my stubborn hair into the pink rods. Considering the time it took to give me a perm, Mom must have thought she was doing me a huge favor. But she wasn't. As far as I could tell, her efforts made me look like I was wearing a Halloween fright wig.

Toward the end of that school year Mrs. Potts brought a radio into our classroom. We listened to a landmark event—the coronation of Queen Elizabeth II. Our teacher acted quite thrilled about the affair, but I thought that getting out of schoolwork was much more exciting than any royal festivities.

1953 was also the year Tommy Benson's father died. Tommy had been at our school since Pam, Nancy, Laura, and I entered first grade. Naturally, after learning about his father's death, we were sad. However, when we realized the funeral was in the cemetery behind our school, our sadness became seasoned with curiosity.

From our vantage point on the swings we watched the proceedings during recess. The procession began at the church across the street and ended at a gravesite, several hundred yards behind our playground.

When the bell sounded, calling us back into class, Nancy protested.

"Oh, no! The bell," she said. "I don't want to go back yet."

Pam nodded. "I don't want to leave, either," she said. "Let's stay a little longer."

When the final bell rang, we didn't move.

After awhile Laura had an idea. "Why don't we pray for Tommy and his father?" she said.

Pray? How do I do that? I may have learned The Lord's Prayer in first grade, but everything I knew about faith came from inspirational songs like "I Believe" that played on the radio.

I decided to use my secret weapon, reserved for those times when social situations turned awkward. And this was, most certainly, one of those times. I swallowed hard. *Do what you always do*, I told myself. *Copy them.*

When my friends lowered their heads, I did, too. My eyes shifted from Pam to Nancy, over to Laura, and then back to Pam again.

Finally, Laura broke the trance. "Amen," she said softly.

The other two mimicked her.

"Amen," I said; then wondered what that meant.

Moments later, we were sobbing in unison. Bawling we were— giant tears from deep within. This time I didn't need to imitate anyone. My tears were genuine. Theirs were, too.

They cried because Tommy had lost his father.

I cried because I didn't know how to pray.

*Here I am as a baby—back in the day when
Mom worked on The Farm. Todd and Kerri
are out front. Gina is next to Mom.*

*Mom is holding Gina at eight moths old.
Gina is adorable. And Mom so beautiful!*

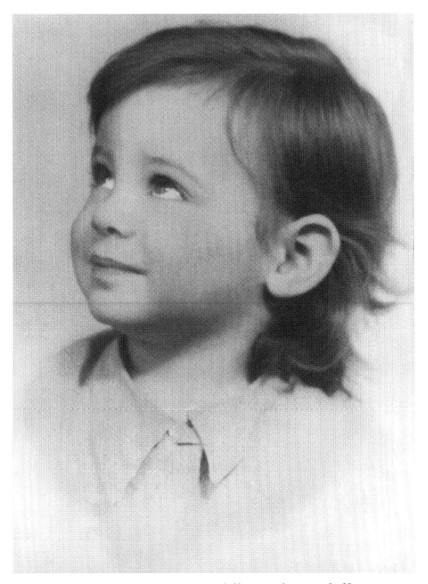

Here's Kerri as a toddler. What a doll!

Todd on the tractor; he's waving bye-bye to his daddy.

Todd with Victor the Goat. So cute!

Gina is holding me. I'm barefoot (we usually were). Kerri is by our side. Notice the barn in the background.

I'm with Kerri and Gina in the Big House yard. Our circular driveway and baseball field is in the background.

I'm with Gina in The Lagoon.

Posing for our first family photo. I'm 5 1/2. Kerri is 10,
Gina 12, and Todd 8.

Here's Todd, in his favorite rodeo shirt, on the swing in our front yard.

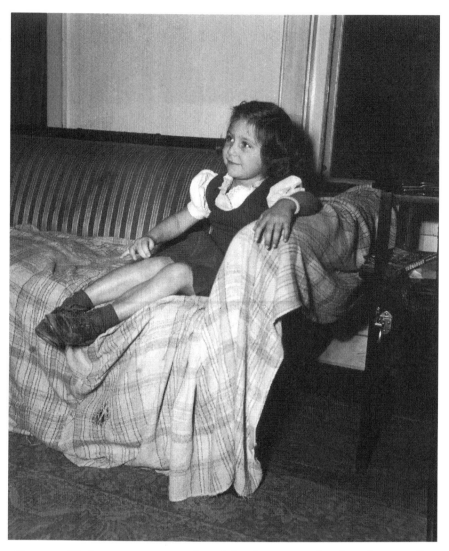

On our living room couch with the coverlet haphazardly tossed about. No curtains on the windows; no pictures or paint on the walls. I must be home!

Cuddling up with Kerri on our living room couch.

The summer before third grade—7 1/2

Several kids from The Farm are sitting on the back steps of the Big House. That's Joey as a toddler, out front. I am (age 2 1/2) sitting behind him. Kerri and Todd are by my side. Gina, Greg, and Julie are in the third row. Elizabeth, Janet, Bobby, and Carter are on the top step.

Dennis with Louis Armstrong in the star's dressing room.
Photograph by Harvey Singerman

It's Easter, and Mom just gave me a perm –in fourth grade.

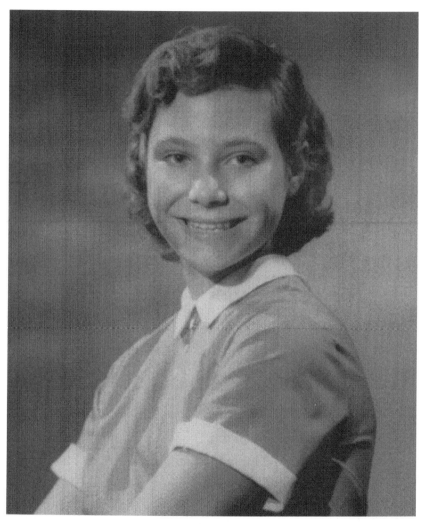

- Sixth Grade -

CHAPTER 33

A few months after Elizabeth got her driver's license, she was in an automobile accident. The Oldsmobile her father had bought her flipped over while taking a sharp turn. It was a triple hazard roll over. First, she was a new driver. Second, she had a fight with her boyfriend. And third, the roads were slick with rain. The car was a total wreck, and Elizabeth looked like she'd been in a street fight.

Catching a glimpse of her bruises, I felt weak and clammy. Then everything faded to black. That wasn't the first time I passed out. Nor would it be the last. Kerri and I fainted quite often.

I remember my first dizzying experience like this: Kerri was standing on a kitchen chair reaching for boxes of cereal above the refrigerator. Without so much as a "Gosh, I'm feeling dizzy," she collapsed on the floor.

Believing that Kerri was faking, I started pouncing on top of her. When I finally noticed her ghost-white face, it was my turn to pass out.

Another incident happened after Todd fell on some glass while playing in the snow.

I heard howling coming from the room Carter and Todd were sharing. Later, that room became Hal's bedroom. Peeking in, I saw my brother clutching his knee and wailing in pain. Blood had soaked through his jeans and dripped onto the floor.

I rushed to the top of the stairs and hollered for help so loud you'd think my brother needed a transfusion. A second or two later, I felt myself going under. At least that time I managed to call for help before passing out.

Then there was the time at the health museum. Hal had been teaching Darla and me different parts of the female anatomy.

Somewhere between the words "vagina" and "menstruation," I became lightheaded. Saliva pooled inside my mouth. On the way down, my body caught the corner of Hal's reading glasses. They hit the floor and broke in several places. When I regained consciousness, Hal didn't act very happy with me. Then again, I wasn't thrilled with his sex education class either.

CHAPTER 34

How does a perfectly good morning turn into a night-mare? I found out in fifth grade. Todd was in seventh; my sisters were in high school. I'd been searching my drawer for an outfit to wear to school when I saw Gina whispering to Kerri. Their faces were filled with distress. I strained to listen.

"She's gone!" I heard Gina say.

"What's wrong?" I asked, afraid to hear.

"You're too young to understand," Gina said, leading Kerri into the hall.

I moved to the doorway and listened.

"She's really gone," Gina said, barely above a whisper. "Go check her closet. All her clothes are missing."

A frightening thought flashed through my mind. *Wait! Does she mean Mom?* I rushed to her closet. Her

201

side was half empty. I dashed back to the hall. My sisters were no longer there.

I couldn't process what had happened. However, I was sure of one thing: I wasn't going to school. I couldn't. Slipping into my parents' bed, I pulled blankets over my head.

This was worse than Mom not being there to tuck me in at night, or only seeing her on Sundays and Wednesdays. I might not see my mother again. Ever!

The day dragged on like it would never end. With every hour, I became more devastated. Finally, the school bus brought the kids home. I joined them downstairs. None of them acted as if anything out of the ordinary had happened. Neither did my father. In fact, he wasn't even available for questions. As usual, he wasn't home from work when I went to bed.

That evening, while I lay in my bunk, events from the day played out on a never-ending loop. When the truth became too much for me, I created several scenarios about my mother coming home. They were all, more or less, the same.

Mom gathered me up in her arms and together we awakened Kerri, Gina, and Todd. Then we raced to Dad's car where he waited to take us away and make us a normal family. Those images were so vivid they almost seemed real.

But when morning came, reality hit hard. My mother was gone. She might never return.

I didn't comb my hair or brush my teeth. I went to my parents' bed, climbed in, and waited for the day to end.

"The bus will be here in half an hour," Edith called up the stairs. "You'd better start getting ready."

"I'm NOT going!" I hollered back, creeping further under the covers.

Alone with my thoughts, I attempted to dispel fear with prayer.

However, my limited knowledge about the subject turned those efforts into begging. *Please bring my mother back home. Please, God. Please ...*

On my third missed school day, I heard a knock on the door of my parents' room. Glancing up, I saw Hal standing in the doorway.

Scrunching under the covers, I placed hands over my eyes and hoped he'd go away.

"I hear you haven't been going to school," he said, plopping down on the edge of the bed.

"I don't feel good," I said in a muffled voice.

"Well, maybe if I tell you that your mother is coming home tonight ... maybe then you'll feel good enough to go to school."

I bolted up and gawked at him. "What?" I said. "Is my mother coming back?"

"Yes. I'll be bringing her home tonight ... about seven-thirty." He smiled, and his tone changed slightly. "I have something for you," he said. He placed a shopping bag on the bed. "Go ahead. Open it. I bought you three new dresses. I think you'll like them. They're different."

I knew I wouldn't like any of his "different" dresses but decided to play along. Perhaps, if I did, he'd tell me more about Mom. Opening up the shopping bag I discovered three of the most hideous dresses I'd ever seen.

"They're different," he repeated, as if that would change my expression from disgust to pleasure.

I cringed. *Pam and Nancy would never wear them.*

"Very nice," I said, managing a pale smile.

They weren't. One was dark blue with a boat neckline that ended in an oversized bow in the back. At least I assumed that's the way the stupid thing went. I couldn't tell the front from the back. The other two were equally disgusting. One was bright purple. The other was an odd shade of green.

"People will notice you in these," he said, trying his best to convince me that "different" was a good thing. I couldn't pretend to agree. Our lifestyle was different enough; I didn't need weird dresses to seal the deal. Anyway, how could he think that new dresses would cheer me up?

"Your mom will be here about seven-thirty," he told me again, heading for the door. "Why don't you watch for her at the dining room window?"

After he left, I jumped out of bed with renewed energy.

The clock on Mom's nightstand read one o'clock. How would I ever make it until seven-thirty? I brought a puzzle up from the basement hoping it would help pass the time. It didn't work. None of the pieces fit, and searching for them annoyed me.

Finally, I heard the school bus arrive. Laughter and commotion filtered upstairs.

"Nita!" Kerri called out, bounding up the stairway. "Mom's coming home tonight ... she's coming home! I heard Edith telling Carter."

"I know," I said, pushing the puzzle box aside, making room for my sister. "Hal told me earlier."

As Kerri sat down, the shopping bag fell off the bed. Its contents spilled onto the floor.

"What's this?" she said, holding up my new blue dress, examining it.

"Beautiful, isn't it?" I said sarcastically.

"Where'd you get that?' she asked, making a sour face.

"It's one of the dresses Hal bought me," I said, turning up the corners of my mouth in disgust. "He thinks it's beautiful. But then, you know how much Hal loves things that are *diff-er-ent*," I said, mocking him.

Skeptically, Kerri lifted an eyebrow "Well, he's right. They are ... uh ... different," she said, checking out the other two. Her eyes shifted from the dresses to me. "But ... are they anything you want to wear? That's the *real* question."

"No! And I sure don't want to wear them to school."

"What else is new?" Kerri said. "Remember when Hal gave Carter those wooden shoes? The other sophomores made fun of him, but he still had to wear them. Poor guy."

The thought of Carter clip-clopping like a little Dutch boy through the halls of the high school was too funny. I had to laugh.

"Oh well ... that's Hal for ya," Kerri said.

"Yeah, that's Hal all right. Hey, I'm gonna watch for Mom at the window later. Wanna join me?"

Kerri smiled. "Yes. Let's wait together. For now, though, we'd better find some food. I bet you haven't eaten all day."

About seven fifteen, Kerri and I went into the dining room to wait for our mother. Exactly why we called that area a dining room I'll never understand. It was a clutter-filled mess with a radio on one wall and buffet on the other. Both were dark cherry pieces that might have been attractive if not for stacks of papers camouflaging their beauty.

A yellow couch, with the stuffing falling out, dominated the exterior wall. That's where we waited for Mom. Kneeling on the couch cushions, we stared out the window, counting cars to make the time go faster. Kerri promised me that before twenty cars went by on the highway our mother would be home.

After what seemed like an hour of waiting, I spun around and sat down in a huff. "She's not coming," I said, pouting.

"It's only been ten cars. I told you ... it's gonna take twenty," she said, keeping a watchful eye.

"She's not coming," I repeated five minutes later. "Even Hal can't bring her back."

"I've counted twelve," she said. "I told you by twenty. Oh wait ... a car is pulling in—"

I bolted to the window. "It's her! It's her!" I squealed.

Edith noticed our excitement and joined us. We ignored her.

As Mom and Hal walked the wooden path to our front door, Mom didn't look very happy.

Edith must have seen something completely different. Her comment dripped with the honey from ten thousand bees. "Ohhh, isn't Hal *won-der-ful*!" she said in her singsong style.

Her comment made my stomach churn.

The front door opened.

"Mom ... Mom," I said, dashing to the living room. "I'm so happy to see you."

"I have to go," she said, heading upstairs. Her face was void of expression.

"But Mom—" I called after her.

"We'll talk about it tomorrow," she said.

But we never did.

CHAPTER 35

The next morning I put on one of Hal's "different" dresses. I chose the green one. It seemed to be the least conspicuous. The last thing I wanted was to draw attention to myself at school.

I was sure that Nancy wouldn't accept a simple excuse for being absent three days. Not without a stern cross-examination. And I was right.

"I told you before ... I was sick," I said, glaring at Nancy. It was first recess. The two of us were on the playground with Pam. "Besides, it's none of your business," I snapped. "I'm going inside."

I'd been at my desk a short while when Pam and Nancy returned to the classroom. Nancy sat in front of me that year. Pam's desk was to my right.

Nancy turned around. "So ... why did you *really* miss so much school?" she asked.

Chin in my hands, I leaned elbows on the desk. I was formulating another story about missed school days when Nancy cut me off with a shriek.

"Your arms! What's that on your arms? For heaven's sake, Anita, don't you ever take a bath?"

"What?" I said, staring at her dumbfounded.

"Your arms ... your arms," she wailed again. "They're filthy dirty." Then she turned toward Pam. "Look, Pam. Look at Anita's arms!"

Glancing down, I almost screamed myself. I was shocked to see brown streaks covering the underside of both my arms. Had water dripped onto them and mixed with some of our "country dirt? Or was it that I hadn't bathed in a week or two?

With so many people living under one roof, the shortage of hot water turned bath time into a once a week affair.

Naturally, that wasn't true for Elizabeth. Hal's oldest daughter was now a senior in high school. And like everything else the girl did, she bathed whenever she pleased.

"Pam ... look at her," Nancy screeched again.

When Pam came over, it was more than I could take. Squeezing my eyes shut, I tried to stop the tears. It didn't work. I crossed my arms and rested my head inside them on the desk. In seconds I was bawling, painfully out of control.

"She's crying! We've got to do something," Pam said.

"Let her cry her eyes out!" Nancy shot back.

That did it! I wanted to get up and run, but had difficulty breathing.

Moments later, I heard footsteps approaching from the back of the room.

"It's Mrs. Jacobs," I heard Pam say.

My fifth grade teacher was different from any I had so far. The others were grandmotherly types. They wore old-fashioned clothes and their hair was pulled into a bun. That wasn't Mrs. Jacobs's style. She was tall, young, and pretty. Her dark hair, worn loose and down to her shoulders, complimented her easy-going persona.

"What happened here?" she asked. "Can you tell me, Nancy?"

Silence.

She tried again. "Pam, Nancy ... what happened?"

Neither said a word.

I felt Mrs. Jacob's hand on my back. "Why don't you come with me, Anita?" she said. "We'll go to the Nurse's Room."

Even though our school didn't technically have a nurse on staff, a small space, overlooking the playground, was referred to as the Nurse's Room. Inside, a cot was positioned under a window. There was a single chair.

Mrs. Jacobs motioned for me to stretch out on the cot. "Be right back," she said. Upon returning, she placed a wet cloth on my forehead. It was cool and her touch felt soothing.

"What happened?" she asked, puzzled.

"Nancy hates me," I said.

"No. She doesn't hate you. You play together every day. She gets a little uppity at times, that's all."

After some coaxing, I told her the exact words Nancy had said.

"I'm sure she didn't mean it," my teacher replied.

Then she looked at me a little more seriously.

"I was worried about you when you missed so much school," she said. "Is everything okay at home?"

That question turned on my waterworks full force.

"It's okay," she said. "You can tell me ... but only if you want to."

I wasn't sure if it was Mrs. Jacobs' comforting touch or kind voice, but I began spilling out the short version of life on The Farm. I told her how different I felt and my jealousy toward Darla. However, I didn't utter a word about my mother running away. That wound was way too raw and much too fresh.

As I spoke, Mrs. Jacobs offered sympathetic nods during certain places in my story. She seemed confused in other parts. I was beginning to think that I'd revealed too much when, in the distance, the bell sounded.

"I have to go now," she said. "Rest here as long as you want. I'll check on you later."

I counted the dots in the ceiling panel and wondered how I'd ever face the kids in class again. Then I stared blankly out the window.

After what seemed like over an hour had passed, I noticed kids on the playground.

I heard the doorknob turn. I assumed Mrs. Jacobs was returning.

Instead, Pam stood in the doorway. "You okay?" she asked, walking toward the cot. "Mrs. Jacobs told me to come see you ... to see if I could get you outside for recess." She smiled. "Listen," she went on, "don't worry about Nancy. She says stuff. She doesn't mean anything by it."

"I know," I said, although I didn't really believe it. "Mrs. Jacobs told me that, too."

Pam held out her hand. "Let's play baseball," she said. "You're up first."

Taking her hand, I smiled. "We'll be on the same team, though. Right?"

"Sure," she said. "Let's go."

That night, when my head hit the pillow, I was haunted by Nancy's words. I heard her tell Pam that I should cry my eyes out. I saw Mrs. Jacobs comforting me. I replayed our conversation, and saw Pam coming in to get me.

Finally, I relived the night before … when Mom returned after running away. I wondered if I'd ever shake the feeling that she might leave again.

CHAPTER 36

Near the end of my fifth grade school year, the worst kid to ever visit The Farm came to live with us. His mother, a Sunday Regular, must have believed that time in the country would be invaluable for her child. He stayed with us for several years.

He was tall and bony, with black horn-rimmed glasses that fit over his long, pointy nose. Oh, and did I mention he was ugly? He also smelled. His stringy black hair was plastered down with so much Brill Cream that he reeked of it. I suppose he thought that if a "little dab would do ya," then a great big glob was even better.

His parents named him Clyde, but I came up with a few other choice words that fit him better ... like brat, jerk, and disgusting creep. I didn't like him. Not one bit.

But I didn't start out thinking about him in that way. Those nasty names were earned.

A month or two after he arrived, Clyde started touching me inappropriately. As if his fondling wasn't bad enough, he would wait until I was walking toward him with my mind in a trance. As we passed each other, he'd quickly grab my breasts or crotch.

Trying to make him stop, I'd kick him in the shins. That made him laugh. I tried "geetching" (our word for pinching while digging into flesh), but that brought on more laughter. Nothing worked. I hated that creep with every fiber of my being.

When that school year ended, as if divinely ordered, a beautiful girl named Beth arrived. She wasn't like most of the kids who visited for the summer. Her aunt once lived with us. Beth was aware of our lifestyle.

We never had a single fight; we only had fun together. During her stay, we choreographed a song and dance routine to "April Showers." We performed for all the kids who cared to watch, plus a few who could have cared less.

While Beth was with us, she and I shared a bedroom in the School House. So did Todd and Clyde. No grown-ups were sleeping there at the time. Who needed supervision, right? That 's' word was simply not a part of our vocabulary.

Beth and I stayed up for all hours, talking, and giggling about her life in the city. The friends she told me about sounded like characters in my *Archie* comic books. She was the beautiful Veronica Lake. Her jet-black hair curled under at her shoulders, just like Archie's girlfriend.

Not long after Beth arrived, Rosa was also dropped off. Her mother, a devoted Sunday Regular, had been loyal to Hal for years. Rosa was a thin, pretty girl with light brown, curly hair cropped to her chin. Freckles were scattered across her nose.

One afternoon, while the three of us walked home from The Creek, we passed by Clyde and Todd.

"I hate Clyde," I blurted out when the two boys were out of earshot.

"Why?" Beth asked, bewildered. "He's a little funny-looking, but he seems nice enough."

"Well," I said, "you don't know him like I do."

"Whaddya mean?" Rosa asked, as we passed the shed. "I've known him for years. His mom and mine are friends. I wouldn't call him my best buddy, but hey, he's not so bad."

"Then you're lucky," I said. "I hate him. When no one else is around, he grabs at me."

"Grabs at you?" they both said, almost at the same time.

"Yes ... grabs at me! He's always grabbing me on top ... or down here," I said pointing. "I hate him. He's disgusting."

"My God," Rosa said. "Did you tell your mother?"

"Heck no! I can't tell her anything. She never listens. Besides, she'd probably make me talk to Hal about it." I made a face. "Believe me ... I won't be telling my mother."

We walked in silence for a few minutes.

When we reached the barn, Beth spoke. "Nita, I'd sure tell my mother if some guy was grabbing at me. I honestly think you should—"

"I know," I said. "You think I should tell my mother. Listen, I'd like to. But I can't."

"What do you mean? You *can't*," Beth asked, looking puzzled. "Why not?"

That was the exact moment I realized that Beth didn't understand quite as much as I'd thought. I loved her anyway.

"C'mon," I said. "Let's jump off the high beam."

"I agree with Beth," Rosa said, climbing the ladder behind us. "I'd tell my mother, too."

"Yeah, well," I said, rolling my eyes. "Things are different here. A lot different."

One at a time we landed in the soft hay below.

We relaxed for a short while; then Rosa was on her feet.

"Hey, I know what we can do" she said. "Let's pants him!"

"What?" I said, wrinkling my nose. "Are you suggesting we pull Clyde's pants down? Are you kidding?"

"It's kinda like that," Rosa added. "It's all about catching him off guard; then grabbing his jeans before he knows what's happening."

We all got a chuckle out of that idea.

Then the smile on Beth's face faded. "It would be funny," she said. "But it might make things worse."

I'd never heard anything like that before, and wasn't willing to drop the subject. "Do ya pull 'em *all* the way off?" I asked.

Envisioning Clyde hobbling around with a pair of jeans around his ankles came to mind. A smile spread over my face. "Pants him?" I said. "Oh, that's funny. Really funny."

The more I thought about it, the more comical the scenario became. I was tempted to tell Rosa that I loved her plan, but decided Beth might be right. "Got any other bright ideas?" I asked.

"I'm thirsty," Rosa said, leading us toward the water spigot near Snowball's stall. "Gimme a second."

When we got there, she cupped one hand under the nozzle and turned on the water with the other. With a popping sound, rusty water sputtered forth. "There must be something," Rosa said, pulling her hand back. She waited for the water to clear; then took a drink.

As water dripped into a gray bucket below, we sat with hands around our knees.

All of a sudden, Rosa stood up. "I've got it!" she said, her eyes bright. "We'll soak his mattress!" She seized the bucket and held it up like Exhibit A in our case against Clyde. "We'll use this," she said, "and soak it good. That'll teach him."

I liked Rosa before, but my opinion of her went up several notches.

"Lemme have that," I said, immediately energized by the idea. "We can do it while he's outside. He won't have a clue it was us." My spirits soared. "Let's do it!"

On our way to the School House, we finalized our plan. Beth would keep a watchful eye at the top of the stairs, I'd dash back and forth with the bucket, and Rosa would stand at the bedpost directing the flow.

"Gangway," my voice echoed through the house. "Gangway ... water coming through!"

Then Rosa hollered, "Pour it here ... where he puts his head."

"Yeah," I said. "Maybe that'll wash away his smelly Brill Cream."

After giving his mattress the dousing it deserved, we headed back to the barn. Along the way we ran into the target of my revenge.

"Whaddya doing with that bucket?" Clyde asked. "Is there a problem?"

"Problem? What problem?" I said, fighting off the impulse to lead a victory dance with my two cohorts.

Rosa grinned. "Well now," she said, leaning in to whisper. "I guess that depends on whether he considers sleeping on a sopping wet bed a problem."

***

For the remainder of that summer Clyde stopped bothering me. I wasn't sure if it had anything to do with my efforts to get even or not. Perhaps it was because Rosa and Beth were almost always with me. In any case, I was free of his obnoxious behavior ... at least for a while.

Almost every day Beth and I entertained the possibility of me visiting her in the city. I wanted to meet the friends she told me so much about, the ones who had lemonade stands and visited each other's homes—just like Archie and his gang.

And so, the Sunday before she was scheduled to leave, I mustered up the courage to ask Mom for permission to visit Beth. I hoped that she wouldn't have to run it past our gatekeeper. But luck wasn't on my side.

"I'll check with Hal and let you know," she said.

I tried to imagine what Hal's reaction would be. He couldn't say no, I decided. He knew Beth's mother, and he knew where I'd be staying. Besides, I'd only be gone for a week. Lots of girls my age went to Girl Scout camp for two weeks.

Finally, my mother returned with the answer. "No, you can't go," she said. "Hal says you have everything you need right here on The Farm."

I was heartbroken. "But Mom, I—"

She turned to leave.

My throat tightened up, the way it always did when I wished to speak up and couldn't. That familiar helpless feeling was in the pit of my stomach.

I wanted to scream, *No, Mom. No. You're wrong! I have nothing I need right here. What I need is a normal family. I need to feel safe without being grabbed every time I walk past Clyde. I need to feel loved, accepted, and wanted. I need to believe that my feelings count. I need to know that what I want matters. And most of all, Mom, I need to feel like I belong ... to someone.*

I wanted to express every one of those feelings, but all I did was stand there frozen in silence, watching my mother disappear behind the screen door.

Beth went home the following Sunday. Saying good-bye, we promised to be friends forever. But I never saw her again.

CHAPTER 37

*T*he fact that my mother had a difficult time forming friendships in her childhood (because her parents moved around so much) may have contributed to her becoming one of Hal's followers. But I often wondered why Mom couldn't stand up to Hal.

As the years passed, my grandmother, feeling guilty about how she had mistreated her daughter, reminded Mom of a childhood incident. Later, Mom told the story to me. In it, her mother pushed her away, only to pull her close again. Similar scenarios played out on The Farm. Perhaps Hal's "push and pull" actions felt familiar. Maybe his behavior was similar to the kind of love Mom had known in childhood.

ELLIE'S STORY – AGE TEN

As the temperature dropped into the low thirties, Ellie's mother randomly tossed items into an old suitcase. While her mother packed, Ellie wept. A wind picked up and rattled the windows.

"Here, you're gonna need this!" her mother screamed, hurling a hairbrush at her daughter. She barely missed the corner of Ellie's head.

"Maybe after everyone makes fun of your straggly hair you'll learn to use that thing. Oh, and you might need this," she added, flinging an old coat in Ellie's direction. "It's cold out there."

A few minutes earlier, Ellie and her mother were playing canasta, laughing and carrying on like best friends.

They lived in an apartment on the south side of Chicago. The rundown buildings were stacked one on top of another. Their place wasn't much, but it was all Jane's husband could afford on his traveling salesman's salary. His job caused him to relocate constantly, often two or three times a year. Once Ellie made friends at school, it was usually time to move again.

Forming friendships wasn't much easier for Jane. Actually, Ellie was Jane's best friend ... her only friend.

"Quit your blubbering and shut your stupid mouth!" Jane howled.

"Let's go!" she barked again. She tugged on Ellie's hand, jerking her toward the front door. Together they trudged down the four flights of stairs and into the cold night air.

Ellie began to tremble. "No, Mommy! No! You can't leave me here! I won't forget to brush my hair again. I'll be good ... I promise. Please don't go. I'll be good."

"You're nothing but a disgusting, spoiled brat!" Jane yelled. "Don't ever come home again!"

Inside the tiny cubicle she called home, Jane slammed the door.

"And stay out!" she shouted, as if her daughter could still hear her. She clicked the lock and shoved the security latch in place.

Jane rushed to the living room window. Staring out, she glared at her daughter. "I said quit your blubbering!" she screamed. "You'll get used to it! You'll see what it feels like to be alone in this damn world. God knows ... I know how that feels."

She ran to the bathroom and slammed that door too. Glaring at herself in the mirror, she grabbed a tube of pink lipstick from the chipped teacup containing her makeup. She pulled off the cap and applied it to her lips.

Then, pressing the lipstick into the mirror again, she meticulously drew a heart around her image.

"It's just the two of us now," she said to the image staring back. "Just you and me. We can do it. We don't need her. We can get along fine without Ellie. And I don't care if I ever see that idiot father of hers. He can't be bothered with us. He's never home anyway. He's always off trying to sell something or other and leaving me all alone to do everything. No! We don't need him, or Ellie. We don't need anyone."

Then her focus shifted. "Stupid! You stupid idiot," she said, wailing at her reflection. "What good are you?"

She selected another lipstick. This time Jane chose a bright crimson. With two bold strokes she slashed an X through the heart she had so carefully drawn.

A branch crashed against the bathroom window. Startled, Jane shook her head. "Where am I? Where's Ellie? Oooh, no! NO! ELLIE!" she wailed.

She dashed into the living room and peered out the window. "Oh God," she said. "What did I do? Poor Ellie must be chilled to the bone."

Her only child was standing under a street lamp, clutching the suitcase.

Jane ran from the window. "I'm coming, darling, I'm coming!" she hollered, hurrying down the four flights.

Ignoring the blast of frigid air, Jane ran toward her daughter.

Arms outstretched, she shrieked, "Ellie! Ell-ieeee!"

"Oh, Mommy! Mommy! Thank you! Thank you for coming back."

Ellie snuggled into her mother's embrace.

"I was so scared! Please don't ever leave me again, Mommy, p-p-please."

"Oh, I won't. I won't. I promise. Come on inside now. We'll brush your hair. Come on. I'll help you."

CHAPTER 38

Once Beth left to return home, Rosa and I started arguing a lot. When Edith had had quite enough, she proposed a challenge.

Kathleen, an expensively dressed Sunday Regular, had recently presented Darla with a beautiful purse. As Rosa and I watched with obvious envy, it must have given Edith an idea.

"Maybe Kathleen will bring you guys a purse like that," she said. "That is, if you can ever stop fighting."

Darla's purse was gorgeous! It was pink with raised red rosebuds crocheted onto the front and back.

Rosa and I decided to give Edith's proposal a try.

After several weeks of admirable behavior, plus a few close calls, our rewards were presented after supper. Before we could get our hands on the goods, we had to watch them get passed around the table. But something was wrong. No one was making any positive comments.

When the crocheted bags landed in our laps, we feigned appreciation. It wasn't easy. Our purses were completely plain. They were beige and devoid of rosebuds or any other decorative feature. Oh well. We shouldn't have been surprised. I suppose Kathleen couldn't allow our gifts to be as nice as Darla's.

***

Several years earlier, Rosa's cousin came to live with us. Although Brenda was well past the baby stage, she slept in a crib in the upstairs hall. She understood some words, but could only utter unintelligible sounds. From my understanding, Hal promised Brenda's mother he could cure her.

Exactly how he expected to cure mental retardation was a mystery. Then again, all the grown-ups did think Hal was omnipotent.

During the time Brenda was with us, Gina and several others were responsible for her care. Toward the end of the summer of Rosa's visit, she and I had our turn. Pushing Brenda in a red wagon was easy. Getting her to play catch with a bouncy ball was more of a challenge.

Still, those tasks weren't nearly as difficult as changing her messy pants when playtime lasted too long.

***

Except for meals with the Sunday Regulars, sweet treats like pies and cakes were seldom offered. However, that summer turned into "The Summer of Cake."

First came Edith's special treat. As I sat at the kitchen table, gulping down a slice of her chocolate surprise, I made the mistake of communicating my appreciation.

"Wow," I said, munching away. "What did we do to deserve this?"

"*You* didn't do *anything*," she said, correcting me.

Ouch! That hurt. She sure knew how to zap all the sugar from a piece of cake. Besides, what was her problem? I'd been doing my chores. Plus, I was taking care of Brenda, even changing her messy pants. That confirmed it. There truly was no pleasing that woman.

Call me bitter, but exactly what had Darla done to deserve her cake? Not a darn thing. Still, I decided to ask her Royal Highness what else she expected of me. She was only too happy to oblige.

A similar incident occurred a few weeks later.

This time it was Hal dishing up cake to all of the children. Correction. To every child except one. Inadvertently, or intentionally, I was being passed over.

Instead of expressing hurt feelings, I kept quiet, hoping that the oversight would be corrected.

"So, who wants seconds?" Hal sang out, in a voice too cheery to be real.

'Hold on there, Fatso. Didn't you forget someone?' I wanted to say.

Instead, I quietly said, "I haven't had firsts yet."

Acting like it was an innocent slight, he offered me a slice. Perhaps his Freudian mind was only trying to help a socially backward child speak up for herself. Who knew?

At the time, I also didn't know the definition of the word "unworthy," but I sure knew how it felt. I had experienced it that afternoon, as well as with Edith's "you didn't do anything to deserve it" treat. Over time, that feeling found its way into my bones, settled in, and found a home.

A third sugarcoated memory happened toward the end of that summer.

It was Kathleen's birthday. You remember her. She was the rich lady who gave Darla the fabulous purse. Rosa and I received the unattractive knock-offs.

Here was the thing about Kathleen. She may have been wealthy, but what she lacked, all the gold in the world couldn't buy. Kathleen and her husband had wanted to have children for a long time. Her inability to conceive was a subject she often discussed with Hal. All of us were aware of the situation.

With that in mind, what kind of birthday cake do you suppose Hal thought was appropriate for her?

Why, one dripping with cruel sarcasm, of course.

Hal instructed one of the women to draw a baby carriage in the frosting on top of her cake. Next to it was the inscription, JUST IN CASE.

Amid snickering, we learned that the cake was made "just in case" the one Kathleen had baked wasn't tasty enough.

So what was the baby carriage reference?

That created a double-whammy. The carriage adorning her cake was a reminder, just in case she forgot for half a second, that she couldn't have children.

Even at age ten, it was hard not to notice that Hal's mean streak was showing.

CHAPTER 39

While growing up, I recall very little interaction with my sister, Gina. That may have been due to our six-year age difference. But, more likely, it was because we both had our own farm-induced trauma. A few weeks before I began sixth grade, even our limited communication was abruptly terminated.

Gina was popular in high school and voted president of her junior class. However, instead of attending her senior year of high school, Gina eloped. Without saying a word, she and her boyfriend drove to a neighboring state that permitted seventeen-year-olds to marry without parental consent.

During their first six months of marriage, Gina and her husband lived in the School House. For all I saw her, she might as well have moved to China. Besides, talking to her wasn't exactly encouraged. In fact, Hal gave me this stern warning: "Whatever you do, don't turn out like Gina."

I couldn't understand why he would say such a thing. Gina was beautiful. And she was brave. I hoped to someday have the courage and inventiveness she had demonstrated by departing from our lifestyle.

Not long after she got married, Gina received a phone call from a high school girlfriend.

When Edith refused to call my sister to the telephone, I did.

As Gina talked, I watched her closely. I wanted to take everything in. With her shoulder-length brown hair and high cheekbones, Gina had turned into a true Ava Gardner look-alike.

Before her conversation ended, practically singing the words, Gina said, "Well ... I'd better go now. I gotta fix supper for my husband."

While I hated losing Gina, she did sound happy with her new life. Who could blame her for running away to get married? Not me. Still, that didn't stop me from getting teary-eyed whenever her name was mentioned.

Mom had no idea why it made me sad, and I couldn't understand why she didn't "get it."

Perhaps it was my way of expressing the inexpress-ible. I mean, let's take a quick inventory: First, Hal de-clared Kerri not fit to talk to; then he insinuated Gina wasn't much better. I must have, at least unconsciously, wondered when my turn was coming. When would I be cast aside as a despicable and horrible human being?

CHAPTER 40

As Rosa's summer visit came to an end, her stay was extended to include the upcoming school year. Rosa was a year younger than me, so when I entered sixth grade, she joined Darla in the fifth grade classroom. That worked out well. I needed school to be separate from anything going on at home.

Here's a fun memory I have from that time frame. It happened after Darla, Rosa, and I watched *Love Me or Leave Me* at the local movie theater. Our favorite part was when the tough guy (played by James Cagney) stormed a singer's dressing room. The singer, Ruth Etting, was portrayed by Doris Day.

When we got home, we couldn't wait to act out that scene. Our version of Ruth Etting's dressing room was the closet in the Girls' Room. It belonged to Darla since Elizabeth was away at college,

Naturally, Darla played the lead. She tugged on her slip, like Doris Day had done. Then she delivered the line, "Had a good look?" to the tough guy (portrayed by me or Rosa). We reenacted that two-minute bit again and again, Rosa and I taking turns storming the closet.

Another scene that occurred during that school year wasn't much fun at all. It happened while waiting for the bell to dismiss us from school. I was in line outside my classroom. Rosa was standing with her classmates across the hall from me. Out of who-knows-where, her mother appeared.

Before I realized what was happening, Rosa was being ejected from the lineup.

"What's going on?" I asked.

Neither one said a word. They simply vanished out the front door.

At home I noticed that all of Rosa's clothes were gone.

Did Rosa's mother have a fight with Hal? Was that why her daughter unexpectedly went back to the city? I had no idea. It was just one more thing that I didn't understand and no one bothered to explain.

***

Our living room once held a stained, green striped couch, hidden under a tattered gray coverlet with a few miss-matched chairs tossed about. Then, somewhere along the way, the old stuff was upgraded to a colonial style sofa, two chairs, a coffee table, and a few end tables. Now here's the shocker: All the items were new, and all were matching pieces.

Yet, in spite of these improvements, the Big House still looked like we were writing *The How-To Book for Hoarders*. And except for Hal's painting project, that started and ended in the living room, the rest of the place never saw a coat of paint. I guess Hal preferred the original plaster coating, even as it morphed into a mural of dirty fingerprints, to a freshly painted surface.

And while most of Hal's followers had left years before, the place I called home was still filled with Hal's family and several of the Children for a Season.

Was I more embarrassed about my home or our lifestyle?

That was pretty much a toss-up. A wave of panic washed over me if classmates so much as hinted they might want to visit. When I agreed to host a Girl Scout meeting, my fears became reality. It wasn't like I had a choice. We all took turns. The inevitable could no longer be avoided.

On the day of the meeting, one of the scouts informed me that she didn't have transportation to my house. I was nervous enough just thinking about the event and now Sandra was causing more stress. After a few phone calls between her house and mine, it was decided that Sandra would ride the school bus home with me.

A cloud of fear followed me the entire way.

As it turned out, Sandra didn't ask any nosy questions. We played outside and then baked cookies for the meeting.

It looked like my get-together wouldn't be so scary after all.

That false sense of security lasted only until two girl scouts arrived at our back door an hour early. There I was, sitting with Sandra at our long kitchen table, with about a dozen others, when Angie and Mary knocked twice; then came inside.

Oh no! I thought. *What will they tell the kids at school about all these people?*

My hope was that before anyone arrived, we'd be finished eating and I'd be greeting everyone at the front door. That way, all anyone would see would be our living room with the new furniture.

The nightmare continued when no one else showed up for the meeting. Even my Girl Scout leader was a "no show." Some of the townspeople didn't exactly endorse our lifestyle. I guess she was one of them.

The evening was spent with Angie and Mary tossing candy wrappers throughout the living room and flirting with my brother. No attention was paid to my feeble attempts at conducting a meeting.

Ah well, Todd did have Mom's dimples and a smile that could charm any girl within fifty miles. My so-called Girl Scout meeting didn't stand a chance.

Needless to say, no scouting business was conducted that night. And there was only one good part to the entire fiasco. It ended.

***

Serious schoolgirl crushes usually begin in sixth grade. At least, that's how it was for me.

Actually, I took cues from Pam.

The boys she chased around at recess became my love interests, too.

In fourth grade, a cute boy with dimples held her captivated. In fifth, no one stood out. But in sixth grade, it was Randy.

The only time Randy ever noticed me was when we were captains on opposing basketball teams. Still, that boy's obvious lack of interest didn't stop my young heart from trying.

Sixth grade was also the year I learned how to dance.

Oh sure, Mom demonstrated steps to the Charleston, and Sonya tried to teach us the waltz. However, those moves had nothing in common with the new musical sounds taking over our airwaves.

The mid-fifties were a time of musical transition. Sleepy tunes, originating from movies and Broadway plays, were gradually being replaced by a new sound destined to storm the nation.

It was the birth of rock 'n roll.

At home, from early morning until the rosary cut in at seven o'clock sharp (sometimes right in the middle of a song), our radio dial was set to WERE.

While local disc jockey, Bill Randall, continued to play songs by Frank Sinatra, the Four Aces, and Patti Page, he started interjecting more upbeat tunes like "Shake, Rattle, and Roll" and "Rock Around the Clock."

I didn't know the dance steps that went with that new beat, but my friend, Laura, sure did. She taught me and the other girls the basics. We improvised the rest.

Laura brought her shiny, red, portable record player (the newest thing on the market) to school, along with a vast collection of 45's. We'd jitterbug our lunch hour away, then have a rock 'n' roll riot all recess.

Later that year, the school installed a jukebox in the gym. It offered an even wider selection of music. I'm here to tell you ... when Little Richard started belting out "Tutti Frutti," I simply had to grab someone's hand and head for the gym floor.

***

My sixth grade teacher, Mr. Mason, was probably somewhere in his early thirties. Rather short in stature, he often displayed sudden outbursts of anger, especially when his class turned into a note-passing factory. We even came up with a special way of transporting our information—through the jaws of a "Cootie Catcher."

The first step was folding notebook paper until it resembled a sailor's cap. Then, to mimic a mouth opening and closing, we stuck two fingers into one slot and a thumb in another. That's where we put our notes. Mr. Mason found these creations about as welcome as cockroaches at a dinner party.

One morning, as he stormed to the front of our classroom, his face appeared to be on fire. "That's it!" he said. "I'm through putting up with this nonsense. Tomorrow's the last day for 'Cootie Catchers.' Tell you what," he added in a calmer voice, "tomorrow we'll have a contest.

247

Whoever has the biggest and smallest one wins. After that, I never want to see those stupid things."

I hadn't heard that much enthusiasm since school was dismissed for Christmas break.

"Allan's gonna win," my would-be boyfriend, Randy, announced. "His cootie catchers are so tiny, his fingers can't fit inside."

"Yeah," I said, "but what if we—" I stopped talking. To get the edge on Allan, I needed to go in a different direction.

Getting off the school bus, I headed toward our basement.

Alongside the wall near our coal bin was a stack of old newspapers.

I grabbed a handful and went to work. I didn't stop pasting and folding until I knew mine would be the largest Cootie Catcher on the planet. And it was. Well, the largest in my classroom anyway.

It was fun sharing the winner's circle with Allan. My achievement, however, didn't win any points with Randy. Ah well ... I tried.

***

In the middle of that school year, Mr. Mason brought *The Cleveland Plain Dealer* into class. He read an article to us concerning surplus food and how the government was dumping it.

I was appalled at the idea and wasn't shy about stating my feelings.

My teacher peered at me over his black-rimmed glasses. "Why don't you write a letter to the editor?" he said. "That's what people do when they disagree with something."

"They do? Really?" I asked.

"Sure," he said. "That lets them know how people feel."

That appealed to me. I jotted down my complaints and presented my letter to him. I didn't expect much to happen. But a few weeks later, Mr. Mason was reading my *Letter To The Editor* in front of the class.

I was pretty excited to see my ideas in print and decided to continue writing. My next correspondence went out to the York Peppermint Patty folks. I wrote about my enjoyment of their patties and how I rode my bike two miles to get them. I also requested the recipe.

Surprised and delighted, I received a personal reply. They did, however, regret their inability to reveal the recipe. Their excuse had to do with producing the candy in large batches. To prove their point, they included a booklet showing a massive mixing bowl.

Not to be discouraged, I formulated my own concoction of sugar, water, and Hershey's Syrup. Then I placed the mixture in the hot sun for several days. It didn't work out so well. But then again, Peppermint "York" Patty wasn't willing to divulge her secret recipe. And the Easy Bake folks weren't around yet.

Soon I moved on to more personal matters, like drafting a letter to the *Dear Abby* column. I'd often wondered what that lady might say about my living situation. One night I decided to find out.

My letter went something like this:

> *Dear Abby,*
> *I'm eleven years old. I hate where I live.*
> *My mom and dad are never home. No one cares about me.*
> *I'm not supposed to talk to my own sister.*
> *Please help me. Signed: Crying in Cheltenham*

Once Abby had my letter, I followed her column faithfully. After reading her advice, I'd turn to the comic section for Dick Brooks' creation of "The Jackson Twins." I loved to fantasize that I'd have their all-American "normal" life, once we moved away from The Farm.

A reply from Abby never came. I guess she thought my lifestyle was perfectly acceptable. One of these days I'll forgive her. I'm sure of it.

CHAPTER 41

I'm not certain if dental bills were paid with Hal's house fund, or if my parents had to come up with the money. I only know that sometimes I got my teeth checked during summer breaks. Following a ride to The Studio with Mom and Charlie, I'd take a bus to Dr. Bennett's office. The summer before seventh grade required several trips.

Mom took me to my first appointment.

Julie (Charlie's daughter) accompanied me to the next one. Her friend, Bonnie, came along. They were going into their sophomore year of high school.

Bonnie didn't have an appointment, but must have wanted to spend time in the city. I didn't mind. It was fun listening to her and Julie talk about boyfriends and high school life.

My time in the dental chair was first.

While waiting for Julie to return, I passed the time by watching Bonnie doodle her boyfriend's name in big, fancy lettering.

"Wow, it's sure taking Julie a long time," Bonnie said after what seemed like too much time had passed.

"Yeah, he does a lot of drilling," I said.

"Do you like him?" she asked.

"No! I hate him!" I said. "He's not very gentle, and he sounds so silly telling me to 'spit-tout' the water."

Bonnie laughed a little. Then she pulled out a tiny mirror and applied coral lipstick to her mouth.

An idea came to me. "Bonnie," I said. "Can I borrow that?"

"I guess so," she said. Then she shot me a suspicious look. "Do you wear lipstick already?"

"No. But can I borrow it a second?"

"Sure. Why not," she said, holding it out.

"This color's too light," I said. Do you have a brighter shade?"

Bonnie glared at me as if I were being a bit too picky. Then she fumbled through her purse. "Will this do?" she asked, holding up a bright red tube.

"Perfect!" I said.

I can't imagine what possessed me to do what happened next.

Perhaps the idea stemmed from when someone scribbled on the walls of our school cafeteria with lipstick. Our teacher made all the girls skip recess and write dozens of times, "I am not the one who wrote on the wall with lipstick."

I figured he wanted to find a match for the handwriting on the wall. Or maybe he hoped that one of us would confess. Most girls were angry to have missed recess due to one girl's stupidity.

Funny though ... when Bonnie went to the bathroom, and I stood on the table with the magazines (lipstick in hand), I didn't think the idea was stupid at all. With great flair, and in the big, bold lettering Bonnie had taught me, I wrote "I HATE YOU" several times across the wall.

When Bonnie returned, I gave her a coy smile. "Maybe he'll get the message that some of his patients don't like him much," I said.

Covering her mouth, she gasped, "Oh no! What did you do? You're gonna get into so much trouble!"

"No, I won't," I said. "He never comes out here. He'll never know it was me."

Bonnie shook her head. She snatched the lipstick from my hand, and rolled her eyes.

When Julie returned to the waiting room, she caught me with a silly smirk.

"What's going on?" she asked. Suddenly her expression turned to shock. "What's that!" she shrieked.

"Nothing," I said. "Let's get outta here."

Mom took me to my next appointment. On the bus ride over, she barely spoke a word. I presumed it had to do with the strange-looking man sitting a few seats away. He was bothering the lady in front of him, threatening to set her hair on fire. No wonder Mom was quiet.

We arrived early at Dr. Bennett's office.

After we sat down, Mom asked if I would pick out a magazine for her.

"Sure," I said, standing up. Then I panicked.

My hate messages ... I had forgotten all about them.

I checked the wall above the magazines. It was spotless. Breathing in a sigh of relief, and then letting it out, I selected The Saturday Evening Post for Mom.

In a few minutes, the receptionist called my name.

I wasn't in Dr. Bennett's dental chair more than a minute when he asked the dreaded question.

"Anita, last week some nasty words were written on the wall of my waiting room. Do you know anything about that?"

For a crazy instant, I considered confessing. Then got scared. "No, I don't," I replied timidly.

As he drilled and filled, I wondered if he wasn't being a little rougher than usual. Or was it my imagination?

Finally finished, he escorted me back to my mother.

"Ellie," he said, clearing his throat, "Can I speak with you a minute?"

Out on the street my mother yanked me close. Fearful, I looked up at her. It was like watching Dr. Jekyll turn into Mr. Hyde. "You couldn't even admit it, could you?" she snapped.

Mom rummaged through her purse. She pulled out a cigarette. Frantically, she tapped it on top the pack. She lit it and inhaled deeply. Then she clutched my hand, tugging hard as we crossed the street.

"Dr. Bennett called me after you left last week. He told me what you did."

I said nothing.

"I asked him to give you a chance to admit it. But you couldn't be honest, could you?"

I remained silent.

"He scolded me ... like it was my fault." She began to cry. "He made me feel like a little girl."

"What did I do?" I said, trying to sound clueless. "I didn't do anything."

"Oh, sure! I suppose a little mouse wrote all those hateful words," she said, jerking me along the sidewalk.

The trip back to The Studio was not pleasant. And I thought the guy wanting to set the lady's hair ablaze was angry! That was nothing compared with my mother's fury.

As strange as it may seem, I didn't receive any punishment. That was also true when (at age seven) I carved my name on top of Mom's beautiful maple dresser. Although she was furious both times, discipline was not the norm. Did she yell at me? Sure. Was I slapped? Sometimes. Made to feel "less than" or non-deserving? Yes, quite frequently. But disciplined? Never. After all, discipline is a form of nurturing, and that was one word we knew nothing about.

CHAPTER 42

*I*n seventh grade, the jukebox blared *"Why Do Fools Fall in Love," "Heartbreak Hotel,"* and *"See You Later, Alligator." I got my period, had to get glasses, and was voted onto the junior high cheerleading squad. It was also the year something terrible happened.*

About a half hour into that school year, one fact became abundantly clear. I couldn't read the blackboard. Having my desk third from the rear didn't help. Everything my teacher wrote came to me in one big blur.

That evening, I left a note on Mom's dresser: "Please wake me before you go to work. It's important."

At the end of the week my eyes were tested. Mom and I poured over available frames. However, making a choice wasn't easy. I hated all of them.

"Come on!" Mom said. "We don't have all day."

After several minutes of indecision, Mom chose a frame with a pinkish tint and hooked them around my ears.

"These are nice," she said.

I thought they made me look sick but said nothing.

"Aw, c'mon," she said, noticing my sour expression. "They're fine."

"Do I have to wear them all the time?" I asked. "I only need them to read the blackboard."

Mom didn't answer for a while. Then she gave her usual response. "You'd better ask Hal."

When my glasses were ready to be picked up, Mom brought them home. I flinched at the thought of wearing them all day and every day. Perhaps asking Hal wasn't such a bad idea.

After getting off the school bus the next day I walked upstairs, set my books and glasses on the sewing machine, and quietly knocked on Hal's bedroom door.

"Can I come in?" I asked meekly.

"Sure, Nita," he said. "What's on your mind?"

I sat down on the edge of his bed near a pile of books.

"I have to wear glasses," I said. "The blackboard is all blurry this year." I paused briefly, staring at him with soulful eyes. "But I hate them."

He looked at me with a fixed stare.

"Do I have to wear them all the time?" I asked.

"Well, sure," he said, chuckling a little. "You're having trouble seeing, aren't you?"

"Only when I need to read the board."

He looked at me a little sideways. "You won't be falling down without them, will you?"

Knowing he was trying to be funny, I let out a small laugh. "No, I can see fine most of the time."

We tossed the subject around until he told me what I wanted to hear.

"Well ... I guess it's okay if you just wear them in class."

"Thanks," I said. "I really don't like glasses."

He giggled as if he could relate. Then he grabbed hold of his reading specs and pushed them onto the top of his head. "Is there anything else, Nita?" he asked, fluffing up pillows behind his back.

I had no intention of telling him about Clyde, the creep who was bothering me since moving in with us. However, soon I poured out my story to him.

"Clyde is touching me," I blurted out. "Down there," I said pointing. "And here," I said, pointing again. "I hate him!" I added with great conviction.

Sitting on the edge of Hal's bed, I waited for him to say that he'd warn Clyde to never, ever touch me again.

That didn't happen.

"Oh now, Nita," he said, "You don't hate Clyde. Besides, maybe he was only trying to teach you something about sex."

What? He can't be serious. I finally get the courage to tell him about that creep touching me, and he tells me Clyde is trying to teach me something about sex!

I stared out the window, disgusted with his lack of support.

Then things got worse.

He started to rub the edge of my T-shirt. His hand moved under it ... then up to my chest.

I froze.

He continued talking ... about what I didn't know. But he kept talking, and his hand kept moving.

I was frozen in fear. I wanted to yell ... wanted to flee.

But I couldn't move.

I sat stiff as a statue, filled with fear, while the man my mother idolized was touching my breasts.

My mind went numb.

Finally, a miracle happened.

The doorknob turned.

It must have startled Hal because he pulled his hand away.

"D-dad?" Darla stammered. "I'm sorry to bother you. Should I come back later?"

I didn't wait for his answer. I vaulted off the bed so fast you'd think a keg of dynamite had exploded.

"Come in, Darla. Nita is leaving now," he said, sounding like the two of us had just finished a game of checkers.

Without a word, I brushed past his daughter.

In the hall, I spotted my glasses lying on the sewing machine.

I wanted to blast them through the windowpane. Instead, I pulled out the bench, sat down, and stared blankly out the window.

My brother and several other kids were playing kickball in the School House yard.

Kickball! They're out there playing kickball while Hal's up here ...

I never felt so angry! I had finally found the courage to tell Hal about Clyde, and what does he do? The same thing, only worse!

It was like my feelings counted for nothing. I was nothing. I didn't matter.

I hate him ... I hate him. If he ever touches me again ...

Mom, Where are you? I need you.

I need you to get me out of here!

For a brief moment, I considered telling my mother what had happened. Then I snapped back to reality. Why bother? She would only listen to Hal's side and never do anything. Then I was afraid that she *might* do something ... like make me talk to Hal about my feelings. Or scold me. She might even tell me that what Hal did was for my own good.

I felt scared, helpless, and utterly alone.

And I felt betrayed. Betrayed by a mother who would hand me to the wolves and not care if they ate me alive.

I retreated to my parents' bed, pulled covers over my head, and wept. I bawled like a baby ... not only for what had just happened, but also for every time Mom wasn't there for me. I never felt more unloved.

No amount of tears could fill that hole in my heart.

CHAPTER 43

*T*ime passed—as it always does—even in seventh grade, *when you feel like salt is being poured into the open wound of your soul. I never forgot what happened that fateful afternoon with Hal. But, like everything else, those feelings remained locked inside.*

I didn't tell anyone about it. Not even Kerri. I felt too much shame. Anyway, she was seldom home. Who could blame her? Everyone on The Farm was told to stop talking to her.

I couldn't tell my mother. I was sure she wouldn't offer any support. And even worse, she might not do a darn thing about it.

Several months later, I was voted onto the junior high cheerleading squad. Although I hadn't expected to make it, voting for myself probably didn't hurt.

Being selected cheerleader was one thing. Figuring out how to get a proper skirt and shoes was quite another.

Nancy didn't make the squad, and let me know she'd gladly take my place if I couldn't get the proper uniform. When Hal drove Darla and me into Cleveland for a movie, I seized the opportunity.

I didn't really like the show. It was *Marty,* staring Earnest Borgnine. Throughout the film I kept thinking how much Hal resembled the guy playing the lead ... same height ... same balding hairline ... same belly.

The guy in the movie was much more attractive though. He didn't have Hal's bulbous nose or giant mole.

When the film ended, Hal played right into my hand. "Who needs shoes?" he asked with a pompous grin.

Since he had recently purchased shoes for Darla and me, he probably thought we would smile and say, 'No, thank you. We don't need any shoes.'

That was one time the short, fat, balding guy had thought wrong.

"I do," I announced, getting it out before fear blocked my ability to speak up for myself. "I need cheerleading shoes."

I summoned my next dose of courage in the girl's department of The May Company.

"I need a skirt, too," I said. "It has to be navy blue, and it has to flare out," I added, quoting Nancy.

"How's this?" he asked, pulling a pale blue skirt off the hanger.

"No! It has to be darker. And that one isn't full enough."

"Wow! You sure are particular. How can I find all that in one skirt?"

I had a sudden fear of going home empty-handed. Then I remembered that Pam's mother was sewing her skirt.

"I can make one," I said, sounding as if doing so would be the simplest task in the world.

I did have *some* sewing experience. I had earned a blue ribbon for hemming a towel in 4-H. Also, Mom had spent time teaching me how to thread our sewing machine, wind a bobbin, and sew in a straight line.

Truth was, most of our time together was spent with me ripping out seams previously stitched together incorrectly. Still, I figured Nancy's threat of replacing me on the cheering squad would spur me on to success. I decided to get the material and pattern while the getting was good. I'd master the "how to" later.

That evening, carrying my packages upstairs, I felt proud of my accomplishment. For the first time ever,

I'd spoken up for myself. But how would I get the project completed on time? When it came to interpreting pattern instructions, the words read like foreign gibberish. Cut on the fold? What fold? I was beginning to wonder what I had gotten myself into. There was only one thing to do. Ignore the enclosed instruction sheet and wing it.

Okay, so my cheerleading skirt had an extra seam because I couldn't find the fold. So what? I had managed to complete the project, and the end result even resembled the picture on my pattern cover. However, I did have one remaining problem. Wrinkles were looming from seam to re-stitched seam.

After waiting (what seemed like) hours for our iron to heat up, my anxiety increased. "What's wrong with this thing?" I asked Kerri as she dashed by. "The dang thing won't get hot!"

"Oh, that's easy." she said offhandedly. "See that black box on the ironing board? Plug it in there. Then plug the black chord into the wall. It'll heat right up."

I'd already done that. Several times.

I tried again. Still nothing.

Desperate, I yelled up the stairs to Edith.

"Just plug it in," was all she said.

Big help she was. Pretending the darn thing had heated up, I slowly moved it over the fabric. Then, convincing myself that all creases and folds would fall out by morning, I hung my wrinkled masterpiece on a wire hanger. That was a good plan. Except that it didn't work.

When morning arrived, so did two indisputable facts: first, try as one might, a cold iron is utterly useless; and second, deep wrinkles won't fall out overnight.

When I arrived at school, Pam greeted me warmly.

"Oh, good. You have your skirt," she said with a smile. "I just hung mine up. C'mon, I'll show you," she said, leading me to the closet in front of our classroom.

At first recess, Nancy acted like she couldn't wait to inspect all the uniforms.

First in line was Pam's. "That's beautiful," she told Pam. "Your mother did a great job." But when Nancy's eyes fell on mine, her face scrunched up in disgust.

"Whose is that!" she said. Then she turned to me. "Anita, is that yours?"

"Of course not," I lied; then shuffled to my seat.

She knew darn well whose skirt it was. And I didn't need her assessment. I was going to cheer regardless of how many wrinkles or seams were showing. Our first game was the next day and I was ready. I had shoes, a skirt, and knew all of the cheers. Hey, I was more than ready.

However, there was one detail I had neglected to factor in. Mother Nature was ready, too. Ready to make her call.

CHAPTER 44

"**M**om! My pajamas! There's a red spot on my pajamas!" I gasped, running toward her in tears.

"Oh, honey, that's okay," she said, giving me an understanding look. "You just got your period."

She sat me down on the side of her bed and wiped my eyes with one of Dad's hankies. "You're a big girl now," she said. "You're all grown up. C'mon, I'll show you what to do."

She grabbed a pad and some sort of belt; then led me into the bathroom. After instructions, her voice got serious, as if about to impart wisdom of extreme importance.

"Today, after school," she said, "I want you to talk to Hal. You need to tell him you got your period."

I was stunned into silence.

"Just do it!" she snapped. "I gotta go. Charlie will be here any minute," she added before rushing downstairs.

I watched as she got into Charlie's car to go to work.

It was early. I went back to bed and allowed my mind to wander.

What is with this day? First, I get my period; then Mom informs me I need to tell Hal about it. What else can go wrong?

Then I remembered.

In the afternoon I'd have to ask Mrs. Snyder for a Kotex. She was the current fifth grade teacher and keeper of the pads. The thought of walking into her classroom and requesting one was not pleasant.

Then a worse problem came to mind. Today was the big game. If Nancy found out that I had gotten my period, she might tell me I couldn't cheer.

For the first half of the day, I was able to keep the news to myself. However, when I walked from Mrs. Snyder's classroom to the bathroom, Nancy must have gotten suspicious.

"Did you get your period?" she asked during recess.

I avoided her eyes. Then timidly replied, "Yes ... this morning."

"Well then, you can't cheer in the game today!" she said, sounding like the voice of authority. "You can't cheer if you have your period."

"Yes, I can!" I fired back. "You can't tell me what to do."

"Well ... we'll see about that. I'm getting Mrs. Snyder."

Within minutes, my friendly foe was back with her mediator.

"Tell her," Nancy said, awaiting Mrs. Snyder's collaboration.

I stared at the fifth grade teacher with pleading eyes. She stared back with a patronizing smile.

"Anita," she said, "Nancy's right. It might be better if you don't cheer today. The first day's always the heaviest," she continued. "There'll be lots of other games. You can cheer next time, okay?"

Her question didn't warrant a reply. I lowered my head, muttered something under my breath, and returned to my seat.

The classroom filled up with students abuzz about the basketball game. As class got under way, our teacher threatened to cancel the game if we couldn't settle down. Most of the kids stared at each other as if to say, 'He'd better *not* do that.' And he didn't.

When the bell sounded, I watched my classmates file out the door. No one seemed to notice that I stayed behind ... my head on the desk, my cheerleading skirt in the closet.

CHAPTER 45

That afternoon, I disobeyed my mother. I had to. What twelve-year-old girl wants to tell any man that she got her period? Let alone Hal.

But as luck would have it, Hal issued a reminder notice after supper.

"Nita," he said, "do you have anything you want to share with me?"

I cringed.

He knew.

I ignored his question as long as I could. "Can I talk with you upstairs?" I finally asked timidly.

When some kids gave me a curious look, I gave them a "none-of-your-business" stare.

In the upstairs hall, I pulled out the bench under the sewing machine. While waiting for Hal, disgusting memories flooded my mind.

I certainly hadn't forgotten the last time I was in his room.

I hoped he might forget about joining me, but footsteps on the stairs told me that it was time.

"Come on, Nita," he said, moving past me.

I followed him; then stood at the edge of his bed. After what had happened the last time, I wasn't about to sit down.

He propped himself up with pillows and said, "Okay ... so tell me, Nita, what's on your mind?"

"I got my period today," I said, mortified to hear such words going from my mouth to his ears. "But ya know ... this whole thing isn't such a big deal. Kerri told me about it when she got hers."

"Now hold on," he said. "Not so fast. Did your mother tell you about sex?"

"Oh, sure," I said, my heart pounding.

Truthfully, I hadn't understood anything that she told me. Mostly, it embarrassed me with her diagrams and words I hoped to never hear.

"You seem nervous. You okay?" he asked.

"Sure," I said, my brain working hard to get him to believe me. "I'm fine. This just isn't a problem. Kerri told me all about it." Then I glared at him, wanting to say, 'Now, can I get outta here, please?'

"I always figured you'd learn about sex from watching the dogs," he said. "But we can talk about this another time."

I headed for the door, but his next words stopped me.

"By the way, have you started wearing a bra yet?"

Now, I was scared.

"Not yet," I said, inching closer to the door.

"Well, you're about ready," he said.

I didn't say a word.

"I'll take you into town for one tomorrow. Don't worry. I won't go into Sandburg's with you. I'll give you money and wait in the car. Okay?"

"Okay," I said. As if I had a choice.

Much to my dismay, Hal made good on his promise.

The next day, the two of us strolled into Sandburg's, the only women's clothing store in town. A saleslady, in a brown skirt and orange blouse (the high school's colors), approached.

Hal put his hands on my shoulders and uttered the words that almost made me cry from embarrassment.

"Can you measure her for a bra?"

The woman nodded; then grabbed a tape measure.

"I'll circle around and pick you up when you're done," Hal said. Then he left.

The woman led me to a rack filled with bras. She began what would be the first in a series of personal questions. "Why isn't your mother here with you today?"

Another lady winked at her and said, "Oh, she's probably working." Then she gave me a fake smile and added, "Your mother works in Cleveland, doesn't she, honey?"

Several strange glances were exchanged as if to say, 'I know what happens on that farm.'

I winced. Why did I need a bra anyway? Couldn't I just wear a T-shirt under my clothes for another year?

As more questions were asked, an angel rescued me.

Instead of wearing wings, she was dressed in business attire.

"I'll help her," she told the other ladies, giving them a nasty look. I suspected that she owned the place.

She put her arm around me and led me into a tiny room where curtains offered a scant amount of privacy. The woman placed a measure over, under, and around my chest. "I have the perfect one," she said. "A beginner's bra."

She selected a box with a picture of a lady modeling a white pointy brassiere. She taught me how to fasten it. Then she took my money, placed my purchase in a bag, and thanked me for shopping at Sandburg's.

"Got it," I said, jumping into Hal's car.

I was relieved when he didn't ask any questions. I'd had quite enough interrogation for one afternoon.

After supper the next evening, Hal placed a large package on the table in front of me. "It's for you," he said, winking. "We're celebrating the good news."

I had no idea what he was talking about.

"This is a special day," he said. "Today we're honoring that you've become a woman."

What? What was he saying?

Then, to my horror, he added, "Nita got her period the other day. She's a woman now."

Oh my God! Now everyone knows.

Clyde sat across from me. His face was drawn into an evil smirk.

All eyes turned toward me. I wanted to disappear.

"Well ... aren't you going to open it?" Hal asked.

"Hurry up," Clyde cut in. "We want to know what's inside."

Hal thrust the package closer to me. "I think you'll like it," he said. "Go ahead. Open it."

Unwrapped, I found myself staring at ... of all things ... a desk lamp.

"It's to celebrate that you're a woman," Hal said, as if that made sense.

I attempted a small "thank you," grabbed the stupid gift and got up to leave.

I heard snickering coming from the kids seated at the table. Then Edith muttered something about how ungrateful I was.

For once, Edith was right. I wasn't grateful. And I never figured out what a desk lamp had to do with becoming a woman.

CHAPTER 46

Like many other experiences, Christmas on The Farm was "different." Instead of being filled with happy memories, that holiday was often seasoned with anxiety, sadness, and confusion.

On the Christmas I was twelve, I didn't venture downstairs with the others. The only thing I could find to wear was an ugly, worn-out chartreuse sweater. Todd was forever teasing me about it. Didn't he know I would have gladly worn something else if I had anything else? I hated that sweater and couldn't bear to put it on one more time ... not on Christmas.

Finally, Mom called up the stairs, "Hey, Nita, if you don't get down here, I'm gonna open up all your presents."

When I still didn't go downstairs, Mom came up to get me. She found some sort of outfit and coaxed me downstairs.

Other less than happy memories included the Christmas mornings when Kerri was being shunned. She received a few gifts those years, but Mom acted like she didn't deserve them.

Still, there were things that made the season happy. I loved Christmas music. My favorite song was Jimmy Boyd's "I saw Mommy Kissing Santa Claus." We didn't own that record, but had several others with grooves worn out from being played so often. I loved "I Want a Hippopotamus for Christmas" and thought "I'm the Angel in the Christmas Play" was hysterical. Another favorite was "Are My Ears on Straight?" That song was about a doll that had been dropped, broken, and filled with the fear of not being good enough. I could relate.

***

During one Christmas season (when I was nine or ten), I made up a little poem. The words were inspired from watching our angel decoration rotate in circles under the heat of eight tiny candles. There was a reflection that I hadn't noticed before. My limerick expressed that image. It also featured a radio jingle that I loved. It went like this:

> *The light that was never orange before,*
> *Hidden underneath the door.*
> *It was really on the floor,*
> *Never been kissed before.*
> *Then one day, it came to say,*
> *I'm very good on sinks and dishes in every way.*
> *And I am very proud to say,*
> *I use Ajax the foaming cleanser*
> *Floats dirt and stains right down the drain.*
> > *Ba-ba-ba-ba-ba-ba-ba! [Sound of water rushing down drain]*

Silly? Sure. But hey, it was something to do. We didn't have television.

***

I don't think that any of the children on The Farm believed in Santa Claus. The grown-ups never encouraged it, and no one taught us to leave out milk and cookies.

Still, every year I dreamed along with Nat King Cole, wondering if reindeer really did know how to fly. I pictured them soaring over our house. I did want to believe so much. Todd always said that it wasn't Christmas until Nat King Cole sang "The Christmas Song." I must admit that's still true for me.

Although we weren't taught much about the jolly fat man, I saw him once at the Statler Hilton Hotel in downtown Cleveland. Mom took me there when I was six.

Santa sat in front of a super tall Christmas tree with several elves. City kids were standing in a line that looked like it might stretch all the way back to The Farm.

When Mom and I finally reached Santa, I wasn't sure of what to say or do. Eventually, a lady, who thought she was an elf, handed me a candy cane and escorted me off Santa's lap. When I rejoined my mother, she checked to make sure that Santa had been properly thanked.

Foolishly, I told the truth.

"I forgot," I said.

Guess what that meant? Yep, one more trip to the back of the line.

Years later, when I relayed that memory to Kerri, she burst out laughing. "No wonder Mom got angry when you forgot to thank Santa," she said. "Her father was playing Santa at the Statler that year!"

Even if Grandpa Schneider hadn't been wearing the beard and red suit, I might not have recognized him. We rarely saw our relatives. Hal discouraged that sort of thing. Long ago, he told his followers to sever ties with former friends and family.

One time (perhaps without Hal's consent), we visited Mom's parents on Grandma Schneider's birthday. Without an elevator, their fifth floor apartment seemed ten stories high. Another time, we had a picnic with them on the lawn of the Cleveland Art Museum. Then one summer day, they came to The Farm for a visit.

When Mom saw her parents' car pulling in unannounced, she ushered Gina, Kerri, Todd, and me upstairs faster than a rocket on takeoff.

While someone escorted our grandparents around the property, Mom gave us a quick once-over with a washcloth and a fresh set of clothes.

They never visited again.

***

My father's family was, more or less, strangers as well. The only time I remember visiting them was on the Thanksgiving before my twelfth birthday. We attended that turkey day celebration with one of Dad's brothers, his wife, and their kids.

I have a scrumptious memory of my Aunt Sofia's home-made cannolis. It was the first time I'd ever tasted that delicious dessert and must have wolfed down half a dozen.

Hal, and all others on The Farm (except my family), were Jewish. So, a knish I knew about. Kugels and blintzes were understood. But Italian sweet treats? Oy vey! This Italian/German girl knew nothing of them.

To which, the grown-ups might have replied, "Italian, Shmatalian! *A bi gezunt* (as long as you're healthy)!"

A bit of that Thanksgiving celebration was captured for posterity. Mom and Dad brought a camera along. Gina, Kerri, Todd and I posed with our cousins. When the picture was taken, Kerri and I thought we were smiling like everyone else. The developed photo showed that we weren't. In addition to not looking very happy, our entire demeanor (stooped posture, blank expressions, and far-away stares) told a million stories of abuse, betrayal and confusion. I guess we couldn't fake it for a photo.

CHAPTER 47

Kerri always personified every quality that I admired. I remember how radiant she looked the night of Cheltenham High School's 1956 homecoming. At halftime, she sat on the back of an open-air, turquoise convertible while being driven around the football field. She smiled and waved like the Queen of England. And so she should have. Kerri had been voted onto the homecoming court. I felt so proud of her that night. Later, I bragged to Pam and Nancy about it.

Dad, however, didn't even watch Kerri's big moment. Neither did Mom.

Oh sure, Mom was there. But her presence was for business purposes only. The Studio had been hired to take photographs for the yearbook.

Shortly after homecoming, a much bigger event was on the horizon.

It began with a simple question destined to change everything about my life, as I knew it. It was a Sunday morning during eighth grade, a few months before my thirteenth birthday.

I was sitting on my bunk reading a comic book when Mom walked up to me.

"Nita?" she said. "I need to talk to you."

The strength in her voice got my full attention. I put my *Archie* down and braced myself. Was she going to tell me she was leaving again?

Then the question came.

"How do you like living here?"

What? Mom never cared how I felt about anything, let alone how I liked living in the Big House. I longed to tell her how much I hated living there, how Clyde had been touching me, and that he laughed when I protested. I wanted to reveal what Hal had done to me and beg her to get us out pronto. But none of those thoughts were conveyed. I remained speechless.

My mind, however, raced on like a runaway locomotive.

Is she really thinking about moving? I doubt it. She never defied Hal before. Why would this time be different?

On and on my mind wandered until Mom broke the silence.

"Go get your clothes and anything else you care about," she said. "Take them over to the School House. We're moving out."

Then she left the room.

For a split second I couldn't move. I expected her to come back and say she had changed her mind.

But she didn't.

As I went through the house, searching for things worth saving, Mom's words became my new theme song, "We're moving out. We're moving out. Glory, glory, Hallelujah, we're moving out."

I noticed a stick of gum I had been keeping to see how long it would take to turn to mold; that went in my pocket. I saw Darla's precious doll—the one with real hair—the one I could never touch.

"She's all yours," I said, hoping Darla might hear.

Then I spotted the lamp, the ridiculous gift Hal gave me when I got my period. I knocked it over and left the stupid thing on the floor.

No good-byes were uttered. It was finally my family's turn to exit without a word ... like all the others had done years before.

We moved out of the Big House that very afternoon. Not that we had far to go. Geographically, our grand move only took us across the asphalt driveway that separated the two houses. Still, we were miles away from Hal's influence, rules, and bellowing voice.

We were outta there!

A few days later, I learned that Gina and her husband would be moving in with us. After so many years, my prayers had been answered.

We were a family. At last!

CHAPTER 48

Life in the School House began with rickety beds plus the living room and dining room sets that Gina and her husband had purchased when they got married. Today that furniture would belong in a "Blonde 50's" collection.

Kerri and I slept in the room where I soaked Clyde's mattress. Todd's room was where Beth and I slept one summer. Mom and Dad used the third bedroom upstairs. There was a small room near our living room that Gina and her husband shared. We had one bathroom; it was upstairs. The entire place, including the dining room and kitchen, wasn't very expansive. After all, it had once served as a one-room schoolhouse.

Who cared? It was big enough. In fact, it was perfect. We all had our own space, not to mention a bathtub that we could use whenever we darn well pleased. Life was good.

Then it got better ...

Yes, Virginia, there really is a Santa Claus. I discovered that while walking downstairs on our first Christmas morning as a family. My eyes must have doubled in size. Bright, colorful packages, in all shapes and sizes, spilled out from under our Christmas tree. Decorative boxes, with colorful bows, were stacked high and wide. Several items, too big to wrap, filtered into the dining room and kitchen. They were simply adorned with giant red bows.

Kerri and I received new twin beds, and I finally got my very own dresser. So did Kerri. Each had three long, deep drawers. Mom also created a bulletin board for us to share. The left side spelled out "Kerri's Korner" in thumbtacks. The right side spelled "Nita's Nook."

Mom was clever ... and funny, too. Who knew? Then again, who knew Mom at all? But the process of getting to know her sure was fun.

Kerri and I weren't the only ones unwrapping presents that day. There were plenty of gifts for all. Santa gave our family a stereo, and would you believe, a beautiful 21-inch, black and white Zenith console TV? It came equipped with, I might add, a pretty fancy remote control.

Now, I may have been the last kid in my class to get a toaster or a television, but I was the first one to hold a magic box that changed channels from across the room.

Naturally, we had to try the remote from the kitchen to see if it would still work. It did. That shouldn't have surprised us. Everything about that Christmas was magical.

In years past, the day following Christmas break had been stressful for me. As my teacher went around the room asking everyone what they got from Santa, my brain got busy making things up. It wasn't that I didn't get presents. I did. I just feared they wouldn't measure up to what others in my class received.

The Christmas of 1956 wasn't one of those years. I didn't need to fabricate a single thing. It was a celebration far removed from the days when Hal distributed gifts to those he deemed worthy enough. What a crock!

Those days were far behind us now. Now my parents were free to show us affection. Now Mom and Dad kept all the money they earned. Now they were able to give us a Christmas we'd never forget. And they did just that.

Later that day, I received the best present of all.

As I was going downstairs, my father was heading up. In the middle of the stairway, we did a little side step to avoid colliding. That's when Dad threw his arms around my neck and gave me the biggest hug.

"Oh, Dad!" I said, hugging him back. "This was the BEST Christmas ever!"

"It sure was." he said. Then he added four precious words I had longed to hear, "I love you, Nita."

"Oh, Dad!" I said, squeezing him tight, "I love you, too!"

That night, stretched out in my new twin bed, all the magical moments of the day replayed in my head. Before drifting off to sleep, my mind wandered back to my most cherished memory of all. It was the moment I knew we were finally free ...

We had just moved out of the Big House. Mom was preparing our first meal as a family.

I was peering into the kitchen cabinets, looking over our odd assortment of plates and bowls. Being accustomed to proceeding with caution, I asked Mom which dishes I should use to set the table.

My mother turned to me and smiled.

I saw a sparkle in her eyes.

As she spoke, her voice was filled with hope and possibility—as if her spirit, too long dormant, had been set free.

"Nita," she said, "you can use any plates you like. We can do anything we want to now!"

PART THREE

BEHIND THE SCENES

We lived in the School House for two and a half years before my family completely moved away from The Farm. The first twelve years of my life contained multiple missing pieces. It took decades to uncover everything that happened beyond the scope of my awareness. Many elements will never be fully understood. Others were revealed bit by bit.

CHAPTER 49

*M*om wanted to leave the Big House long before we actually did. Dad wasn't willing. When nothing else worked, Mom packed up her clothes and fled. Her travels only took her as far as a vacant apartment above The Studio. In fifth grade, I only knew that my mother was missing for three days. It would be many years before I became aware of the details, as well as the truth, behind many other events.

The catalyst for our getting away from the Big House had been Kerri finally telling Mom what happened that night in the theater ... the night she was molested at twelve years old.

Somewhere near the bottom of a bottle of Jim Beam, my mother found the courage to stand up to the man who had once ruled her life.

She told him that she knew what he had done to Kerri, and threatened to go to the police.

"You don't want me touching your daughter," Hal informed her offhandedly. "Fine. I won't touch your daughter."

That was all he had to say on the subject.

But my mother wasn't done talking.

Mom reminded her former guru how many years she and Dad had worked with very little pay. She also refreshed his memory about his promise to give them land after twenty years of faithful service.

"Well, it's almost been twenty years," she told him. "Nick and I want our share."

In the end, Hal gave my parents several acres of property that he had obtained in another part of town. He also signed over half of The Studio to them. The other half went to Charlie.

The reason Kerri had been shunned for two and a half years remained a mystery to me for a long time. When it was happening, Kerri didn't understand it herself. Over the years, as certain facts became known, she was able to put various pieces together and make some sense of it.

To the best of Kerri's understanding, Hal got angry with her because, upon returning home from the theater, she climbed the stairs and hurried into her bunk, instead of his arms.

That night, Kerri violently punched her pillow saying, "I hate you, I hate you; I hate you!"

A minute later Kerri's conflicted mind remembered how Hal had once pampered her, spoiled her, taught her how to cook, and praised her in front of others. The next time she punched her pillow, she said, "I hate you, I hate you, I hate you ... I love you!"

Kerri despised Hal for everything he had done that night, but she couldn't forget how he had once treated her like she was the most amazing girl in the world.

To pay Kerri back for avoiding his further advances, Hal told everyone on The Farm to stop speaking to her. He never revealed why. His commands required no explanation. He was The Boss. Ours was not to question why. Ours was to follow his rules over reason and listen to his advice over common sense.

So Kerri was punished ... not for anything she had done wrong. She was punished for what she had been *unwilling* to do. And part of that punishment involved telling everyone on The Farm to ignore her.

The truth was, Kerri would have gladly talked to Hal again. She was more confused than angry, more shattered than hurt. If only he had given her a kind word, a warm glance, a tender touch, she would have been happy to start talking to him. She probably would have forgiven him. She may have even convinced her confused mind that the night in the theater had never happened.

A part of Kerri had died that night, and she desperately wanted it back. A part of her psyche *needed* it back. She needed Hal to adore her again. She wanted him to come to her.

But that didn't happen.

That *couldn't* happen.

That wasn't Hal's modus operandi.

Hal wanted Kerri under his wing of control, right where he expected everyone to be. But to have the upper hand, he needed her to come to him. To accomplish that, he used various tricks of manipulation.

Kerri was in seventh grade when her nightmare began. Until then, she had only the highest regard for Hal. She loved him even more than her own father. To her, Hal was wonderful. He was perfect. He was God.

Hal coddled Kerri and raised her status to the Golden Girl of Erehwon. In return, she idolized him. His adoration set her apart. However, in an instant, all of that came crashing down.

It was years before Kerri told me what happened that night in the theater, and everything that occurred afterward ...

KERRI'S STORY

As actors and actresses portrayed characters on the movie screen, Kerri's world imploded. She couldn't process what was happening. She knew what Hal was doing was wrong. But this was Hal. He couldn't be wrong. She was puzzled and devastated. Nothing made sense.

Later, when Kerri returned home, she wasted no time jumping out of Hal's car and retreating upstairs to her bunk. She lay awake for hours trying to make sense of what had happened. From past experience, she knew she couldn't tell her parents. They would never go against Hal. And even worse, they might say Hal was right for doing what he did. With no one to tell, all the horror remained within.

Several months prior, Hal had been teaching Kerri how to cook. Making supper had become something she especially enjoyed. However, on the afternoon following that night in the theater, Hal didn't seem to want Kerri to experience *any* form of joy.

When he noticed her starting to prepare supper, he walked up to her with an ice-cold gaze. "Give me that," he said, yanking the frying pan from her hand. "You don't need to be cooking anymore."

Kerri received the silent treatment the rest of seventh grade, all of eighth grade, her freshman year, and into her sophomore year of high school. Hal paid no attention to her, and most people on The Farm behaved like Kerri didn't exist. Her mother and father rarely spoke to her. When they did, their attitude was cold and unloving.

Then, during Kerri's sophomore year, she was surprised when her father picked her up after cheerleading practice. It was three weeks before Christmas. Her father seldom talked to her at home, but he had plenty to say when she got into his car that afternoon.

"We won't be buying you anything for Christmas this year," he said. "We just don't have the time."

He then stuffed a fifty-dollar bill into Kerri's hand. She stared at him dumbfounded.

"What's this for?" she asked, examining the money.

"You can use it to buy your own Christmas gifts," he said.

Kerri was too stunned to say anything.

The longer she thought about the money, the more enraged she became.

Before school the next morning, Kerri slammed the fifty dollars down on her mother's dresser. "Here, take this," she said. "I don't want any presents if *you* can't buy them for me!"

"What?" her mother said, poised to strike Kerri.

A verbal assault began. "You're a terrible girl," she said. "Hal treated you like a princess all these years. Now you think you're too good for him ... won't even talk to him. You're nothing but an ungrateful, spoiled brat!"

Kerri ran from the room in tears. She wanted to reveal what Hal had done in the theater, but past experience had taught her that her mother wouldn't listen.

Later, sitting at her desk in study hall, Kerri never felt so alone. She thought about how Hal was like a master fisherman, baiting his followers with charisma, compliments, or whatever lure he deemed necessary. However, as soon as they did anything to displease him, he would hurl them back into the sea. That's what he had done to her.

Kerri didn't want to get hooked again, but she missed the attention she had received all those years. She now had a hate/love relationship with Hal. She wanted to feel special again, but not on his terms. Not the way he had been in the theater.

Kerri thought about how her mother had acted earlier that morning, and the money her father had given her to buy her own Christmas presents. In her heart, she knew that Hal was behind all of it. She feared that if she didn't resolve the situation with him, he would turn her parents completely against her. She couldn't bear the thought of that happening.

Before study hall ended, Kerri came to a conclusion. She decided that even if Hal turned away from her, she was going to initiate some sort of conversation with him.

After school that day, Kerri took a resigned breath, strolled up to Hal, and started talking. He was cold and indifferent at first, but soon warmed up to her. Their relationship returned to where it had been before everything went horribly wrong.

And just like that, Kerri became the Golden Girl again.

Later that evening, her mother hugged Kerri's neck. Then in a sugary-sweet voice said, "Well, I hear you're quite the talker."

Hearing those words, Kerri knew that Hal must have told her mother that she had started talking to him again.

How did she know that?

Simple. She understood the "ins" and "outs" of The Farm. She knew exactly why her mother would be relieved and delighted that she was talking to Hal. The truth was, her mother *needed* Kerri to start talking to him for her own survival ... so *she* wouldn't be on the "outs" with him.

Talking to Hal was important to all grown-ups on The Farm. Anyone who made Hal angry was considered on the "outs" with him. None of them wanted that. Being on the "outs" meant being mistreated, being ignored, being shunned. Additionally, any child that was not in Hal's good graces was a reflection upon their parents, thus diminishing his favor towards them.

Hal was known to give high praise for scholastic accomplishments. So, when Kerri received a perfect score on a geometry test, she couldn't wait to share the news with him.

After school, she found him in the basement.

"Guess what happened today?" she said, rushing up to him, filled with excitement.

"Y'know," he said nonchalantly, "I've been thinking about that night in the theater." He paused. "Do you remember that night?"

Kerri glared at him, shocked that he would be bringing up that subject. She thought they had their special relationship back. But now ... now he was talking about that horrible night.

"Well, yeah, I remember," she said cautiously.

"I was only trying to help you that night," he said. "You see, after a girl has sex, she becomes a better dancer. Girls who have sex feel so free with their bodies that they glide across the dance floor with ease."

He formed a circle with his index finger and thumb. Then pushing the index finger from his other hand in and out of the circle, he said, "This is how it's done. And some people do it because it's fun." He gave her a creepy grin. "And that's what I was going to do for you."

Kerri cringed. She turned to leave.

For the first time, she saw the man for who he really was. Once again, insanity had tried to rule, but this time Kerri knew better. She wanted only one thing—to get away from him.

Halfway up the stairs, Hal surprised her with another shocking question. "Did you get your period yet?" he casually asked.

Reluctantly, she said, "Yes."

"Oh!" he said. "Then it's too late."

Kerri presumed he was insinuating that it was "too late" because after she got her period she could get pregnant.

"You'd better believe it's too late," she said under her breath.

Before she reached the landing, Hal called up the stairs, "Hey, Kerri, what was it you wanted to tell me before?"

"Oh, nothing," she said.

Then, not so accidentally, Kerri let the basement door slam shut.

From that point on, Kerri never spoke a word to Hal. School became her haven. She was home as little as possible. On the few days that she didn't have after school activities, Kerri went directly upstairs. When she noticed Hal's car in the driveway, she didn't come down for supper. She would rather not eat than sit in his presence.

Once Kerri completely stopped talking to Hal, her relationship with her parents was worse than ever.

On her sixteenth birthday, her mother gave her a camera. "Here, I got this for you a while ago," she said, holding out the gift. "But you don't deserve it now that you aren't talking to Hal."

Kerri was speechless.

"Take it!" her mother said, pushing the Kodak into Kerri's hands.

Kerri couldn't be fooled again. She recognized this to be yet another ploy. She was done talking to Hal no matter what trick was used. She no longer wanted, or needed, that kind of love.

Kerri kept the camera. Since no one taught her how to operate the features, some pictures turned out blurry. She didn't care. Kerri could cope with photos slightly out of focus. She couldn't survive without her dignity.

People at school liked Kerri. She was a cheerleader during all four years of high school. However, Mom and Dad never—not even once—went to watch her cheer.

Hal even tried to take the joy of cheering from Kerri by having Mom tell her the activity would make her legs too muscular. Kerri refused to listen to such nonsense. She cheered anyway.

Many years later, Kerri came to understand that for most of her childhood Hal had been preparing her (with his favor) for that moment in the theater.

She also realized how much she had been manipulated after the theater incident. It was later confirmed that Dad giving her the fifty dollars had been Hal's idea. Likewise, the anger Mom demonstrated when Kerri returned the money, had been part of Hal's trick to make her feel abandoned. No doubt, he thought if Kerri experienced total rejection from her parents, she'd have no choice but to turn to him.

For the love and understanding being denied at home, Kerri often found refuge with Sonya at the Steel House. So did Gina ... when she fell from grace for running away to get married.

Kerri learned to live with her pain. But after that night in the theater, she never felt like the same person again.

CHAPTER 50

*O*ver *fifty years passed before I knew the steps Gina took when Mom ran away. She was sixteen at the time.*

GINA'S STORY

After school, Gina walked to the drug store with Elizabeth. She planned to make telephone calls on the payphone until she located someone with information concerning her mother. First, she called The Studio. However, if Charlie knew anything, he wasn't talking.

"Who else might know?" Gina asked Elizabeth. "Who else?"

"What about your grandmother?" Elizabeth offered. "I'll bet your mom went back home."

Gina took the receiver off the hook and dialed "0." She waited for the call to connect.

"Operator, may I help you?" a friendly voice said.

"I need to call my grandmother," Gina said frantically. "I don't know her number. She lives in an apartment in Cleveland ... on the West side I think. No, I don't know the address, but her last name is Schneider ... first name is Jane. I don't know Grandpa's first name."

The connection was made.

"Grandma? Hi, Grandma. It's me, Gina," she said. "I know we haven't visited you for awhile, but I need to ask you something important."

"What is it, Gina? Is everything okay?"

"Do you know where Mom is?" Gina blurted out. "I mean ... have you seen her?"

"Gina! What's wrong?"

"Nothing. Everything's fine." She took in a quick breath and let it out. Gina didn't knew her grandmother very well and felt awkward asking her such questions. "It's just that I didn't see Mom today. I'm sure she's okay, but I was wondering if maybe she came to visit you."

"No, Gina. I'm sorry. I haven't seen your mother in a long time. Did you call The Studio? She's probably there."

"Oh yeah. Work. I forgot," she lied. "Yes, Grandma. I'll try there. I'm sorry to have bothered you."

As she hung up the phone, Gina began to sob. She felt certain that no one in the Big House would even acknowledge that her mother wouldn't be coming home that night.

And she was right.

After learning of this event, I was so proud of Gina. I felt the same toward Elizabeth. Had I misjudged her all those years? She didn't have to support Gina, but she did. What else about Elizabeth didn't I know? I'm sure there was a great deal.

Sadly, as the years passed, I found out that Gina had not escaped Hal's sexual misbehavior. Following an afternoon of swimming in a nearby lake, Hal told Gina to sit close to him in his car. Then, with several kids in the back seat, he fondled her. Gina was thirteen.

CHAPTER 51

When Debbie died, most men on The Farm were thirty-five. The women were two or three years younger. Hal was forty-five. The Group had been living in the country for eight years.

I was only three and a half when Debbie passed. I barely remember her. However, I do recall one woman with a nurturing touch. From everything I've heard, I'm sure it was Debbie.

A shroud of mystery always surrounded her death. People spoke of it in hushed tones, and details were never explained. It took several decades for me to put the pieces of that puzzle together and learn, what I have good reason to believe, was the truth.

Debbie's Story is not meant to portray events exactly as they occurred, but rather to suggest the essence, to the best of my knowledge, about what transpired.

DEBBIE'S STORY

In early spring, the entire farm burst forth with new life. The fields were blanketed with bluebells, butter-cups, and countless other wildflowers. Colors became more vibrant, and the clean country air smelled even fresher.

The day before Debbie died was that sort of day.

Debbie and Ellie had been best friends since they met in Hal's study group. They grew up in the city and ap-preciated the freedom that country life offered. One of their favorite chores was calling in the cows from the pasture. As the clock ticked away on the final days of Debbie's life, they took Ellie's daughter, Kerri, along. There wasn't anything unusual about that. Calling in the cows was a nightly ritual for the three of them.

"Come on, Debbie," Ellie said, checking the position of the sun. "It's getting late." She bent down and hoisted her daughter onto her shoulders, piggyback style. "Oh! I love this time of year," Ellie said, taking in the natural beauty of the season.

"Me, too," Debbie said, grabbing a cluster of purple lilacs. She handed the bunch to Kerri. Then their nightly songfest began. It continued all the way to the pasture and back.

When they returned to the Big House, chores completed, Kerri was distracted by a group of kids carrying Mason jars with tiny holes in the lids.

"Look!" Kerri squealed. "They're catching lightning bugs. See ya." She said; then dashed off to join the others.

The two women entered the Big House through the back screen door.

Ellie turned to Debbie. "Oh dear," she said. "I just remembered it's my turn to cook tomorrow."

"You're right," Debbie said. "We'd better start planning."

With pencil and paper, Ellie sat on the vinyl bench under the kitchen window.

Debbie selected a chair across from her.

"Okay, what sounds good?" Ellie asked, reaching for cigarettes and matches.

As the women sat contemplating supper choices, a car pulled into the driveway.

Ellie pushed open the café curtain. "It's Ted!" she said. "What's he doing here? He never comes home this early."

Debbie looked bewildered. She rushed to the window. "What's he doing here," she said.

Minutes later, Ted entered through the screen door.

"Well, speak of the devil," Ellie said.

Ignoring Ellie's remark, Ted walked over to his wife. "Debbie, we need to talk. C'mon," he said, leading her toward the library.

Despite the fact that books had never lined the walls of that room, it was still referred to as a library. Actually, it was a sparsely furnished area that always functioned as someone's bedroom. A full-size bed and nightstand lined one wall. A chest of drawers was on the other. One light bulb, twisted into an uncovered ceiling fixture, illuminated the room.

"Sit down," Ted said, guiding her to the bed.

"What's wrong?" Debbie asked, sitting beside him.

"Everything," he replied. "It's not working, Debbie. *We're* not working."

Debbie's eyes widened as his words settled in. "Ted! You can't be serious! I know you hate your job, but—"

"It's not that, Debbie."

"What is it then? Tell me," she said, exasperated. "What *is* the problem, Ted?"

"I'm sorry, but—" He turned away from her. "I just don't—"

"You don't what?" Debbie shot back.

His voice was barely audible. The words came out in a rush. "I don't love you," he said, sounding relieved. "Debbie, you know as well as I do, we only got married because Hal said we should. But now—"

"Now what?" she said with an angry edge.

"Now I want more."

"I can't believe this!" she protested. "You're hardly ever home ... not even on your day off. I never know where the hell you are. Now you come home and—"

Ted shot up and started pacing.

For quite a while neither spoke a word.

Finally, Ted stood in front of her. "What's the sense of talking? I want a divorce," he blurted out. "I can't live like this anymore. I can't live with a woman I don't love."

"Oh ... so that's it," Debbie said, glaring at him suspiciously. "You love another woman, don't you? That's what this is about."

He looked down at the wooden floor, examining the scuffmarks. His voice was flat. "It doesn't matter," he said, swallowing hard. "We had problems long before this."

"Who is it?" Debbie shrieked, "Where did you meet her? I have a right to know."

"Listen, Debbie, I've already decided. It's over."

He headed toward the door.

"No, Ted! You can't leave. Did you talk to Hal about this? He's not gonna like it. But you need to talk to him."

"Hell, no! I'm not talking to Hal about this. I'm not like you. I don't run to that man with every little thing." His eyes narrowed. He reached for the doorknob. "That's what *you* do. That's not what I do."

"But you should. He can help."

"I'm done talking to Hal," he protested. "I don't need his opinion. I know what I want."

She got up, hurried to him, pleading. But, Ted—"

"I'm leaving now," he said.

As Debbie cried, Ted quietly turned the doorknob.

Debbie stared at the door as it closed behind him. Seconds later, the screen door slammed.

Ellie crushed out her cigarette and ran toward the library. She pounded on the door. "Debbie? Debbie, what's going on?"

Debbie didn't answer.

Ellie tried to force the door open. It wouldn't budge. "Debbie, please! Please unlock the door!"

Debbie's voice was emotionless. "It's okay. I'll talk with Hal in the morning. Don't worry, Ellie. I'm fine."

Sonya was in the living room. Hearing the commotion, she rushed toward Ellie. "What's the matter?" she said with concern.

"Nothing. It's nothing. Debbie is going to bed early, that's all."

"Going to bed? At this hour?"

"She's tired," Ellie said flatly. "She's just tired."

The next morning Debbie got up early. Skipping her usual coffee and conversation, she went directly upstairs. Softly, she knocked on Hal's door.

"Can I come in?" Debbie said timidly.

"Sure, Debbie. I was just reading. How are you?"

"Not very well," Debbie said, entering his room. She closed the door, walked over to the other side of the bed, and sat.

"So," he said. "What's wrong? What brings you here so early?"

"It's Ted," she said. "Ted is leaving me."

"He's leaving you? That's crazy. He can't leave you."

"He's found someone else. I think he's got a girlfriend."

"That's ridiculous. Tell him to get in here after work. I need to have a little talk with that guy."

"I did. I told him. I tried to get him to see you last night." Tears formed in her eyes. Her head went down. "He's probably with her right now."

"Debbie, this is serious! You'd better think of a way to get your husband in here."

"But I tried," she repeated.

"Then try harder!" Hal sat up straight and glared into her eyes. "Debbie, if Ted leaves you ... well, you know what that means. If he leaves The Farm, you're gonna have to leave."

"What? No! I love it here."

"I know you do. That's not the point." He stared at her even more intently. "That's my rule. That's been my rule since we moved here. No single women can live on The Farm. You know that."

"Hal, I can't leave. Where will I go? What will I do?"

"I suggest you take a walk. You'll feel better," he said. "You need time alone."

"But Hal—"

"You can go now," he said sternly. "We're done here. There's only one thing you need to do. Get your husband to talk to me."

"But I did. I think I did everything I could."

"Debbie!" he said, yelling now. "How many times do I have to tell you? Don't think! Just do what I tell you. Now get out of here!"

"But, Hal," she pleaded one last time.

He rolled his eyes and picked up the book he was reading prior to her intrusion. He waved his hand dismissively.

Debbie reluctantly got up and walked downstairs. As she passed the women sitting at the kitchen table, her face was void of expression.

Ellie called after her, but Debbie kept walking.

Her gait was a shuffle; her posture made her look small.

Ending up in the pasture, Debbie sat and leaned against the oak tree. The rope hanging from a high branch made her think of her children. In her mind's eye, she saw Bobby and Janet grabbing onto the rope. Swinging high up in the air, they jumped off. Then they scurried to the back of the line with the others.

She thought back to the day when a call came from the adoption agency.

"There are two children who lost their mother in an automobile accident. They need a home," Debbie heard.

That was six years ago.

Debbie had wanted to get pregnant for quite some time. She was afraid that she'd never know the joy of even one child. But soon she was coming home with two.

Those memories brought tears to her eyes.

In the distance, Debbie saw The Creek. She ambled down the hill and knelt beside the water's edge. She picked up a pebble and gave it a gentle toss. Watching the ripples spread toward the shore, she began to sob.

When Debbie didn't show up for supper, Ellie set out to find her. She discovered her friend staring off into space, wide-eyed and desperate, like a person in shock.

"Come on, Debbie ... let's go," Ellie said, putting an arm around her friend.

When they arrived at the Big House, the other adults were at the kitchen table. Most of them were smoking and drinking coffee.

Debbie walked past them without a word. She entered the living room and sat down at the piano. Leaning her head back, she closed her eyes, and began playing a hymn she learned as a child.

When Ellie brought her a plate of food, Debbie didn't seem to notice.

A few hours later, everyone except Debbie, went to bed.

For a while longer, the Big House was filled with music.

Around midnight, the house became quiet.

Then the banging started.

Nick was the first one out of bed. Rushing in the direction of the noise, he headed downstairs.

Hal was in the dining room, sitting quietly at a card table. An unfinished puzzle was spread out before him.

The banging continued.

"What the hell is going on?" Nick said. "What the devil *is* that?

More banging.

"It's Debbie," Hal said calmly, pointing to the library.

"My God, what's wrong with her?"

"She'll be fine," Hal said. "Don't worry. I'm taking care of everything."

'What do you mean you're taking care of everything?' Nick wanted to say. 'She's in there banging her head open while you're putting a puzzle together!'

"Don't you think we should call a doctor?" Nick said instead.

"If she wants a doctor, let her tell me she wants one," Hal said flatly.

"But she must be sick. She needs help."

"I said don't worry about it," Hal snapped.

The banging was heard throughout the night.

Ellie and several other women were desperate to comfort Debbie, but Hal wouldn't allow it. He proclaimed himself the only one permitted to see her.

Eventually, the banging stopped.

After a doctor was finally summoned to The Farm, Debbie was pronounced dead.

Later that evening, Hal brought the adults into the kitchen for a glass of wine. Then, to symbolize the end of one thing and beginning of another, they crashed their empty glasses against the kitchen wall. The next day, all the children were sent to school as if nothing had happened. Even Debbie's children attended classes—Bobby in fourth grade and Janet in second.

Gina and Bobby shared a classroom. All morning Bobby looked distraught. During class, he rested his head on the desk. That afternoon, he refused to go to recess. Their teacher, realizing that Gina was somehow connected to Bobby, asked if she knew what was troubling him.

Gina explained, as best a confused nine-year-old child could, that his mother had died the night before.

Janet was equally distressed, but no arms consoled her.

Kerri, Gina, and the other children were also sad.

However, the most nurturing women on The Farm couldn't be found. She was gone forever.

In time, Ted came to pick up Bobby and Janet. Debbie died that night after ingesting rat poison. As Debbie beat her head against the wall, presumably, she was trying to end the unbearable pain.

Or could it have been a cry for help?

CHAPTER 52

Barbara was one of Hal's faithful followers. She idolized Hal since his study group days in Cleveland. She didn't join The Group when they moved to the country. Instead, she drove out to The Farm almost every Sunday. Barbara rarely had much to say to the children. But her son, Bernie, sure did.

Bernie was a scrawny child, a year younger than Gina, who blossomed into a klutzy teenager. He had a nose that looked more like an eagle's beak than anything else. That didn't matter to us kids. Whenever he visited, his quick wit and funny stories kept us constantly entertained. Some of the grown-ups said that Bernie struggled with a poor self-image, but they couldn't convince me and the other kids of it. We enjoyed him thoroughly.

Bernie's Story is not meant to portray events exactly as they occurred, but rather to suggest the essence, to the best of my knowledge, about what transpired.

BERNIE'S STORY

Bernie wasn't the most attractive boy in the world. In fact, he was downright homely. But there was this thing about Bernie. His nose. Oh, how the kids on The Farm loved that nose! It was long and hooked around ... the perfect nose to joke about. But the kids never did. It was Bernie who made the jokes.

"Oi, I've got such a nose ... such a nose!" he would say, thrusting it forward for review. "Doncha think it's a work of art? So small and cute, right?"

And, while the kids giggled, he'd strut around ... his nose high in the air ... until every kid agreed that, yes, he did have a rather spectacular nose. Then he'd slip into a funny story or give a popular song a comical twist. The kids would smile and then laugh. They laughed until their sides hurt.

"Hal, I wish Bernie could feel as confident at school as he does here," Barbara said one Sunday. "He gets along great with these kids, but around his high school friends, it's a different story."

"Well, I like him," Hal said. "He's so bright. I'd love to see him working alongside Charlie," he said smiling. "You don't live very far from The Studio. Bernie could take a bus over after school."

"Sounds like a great idea. Do you need extra help?"

"Well now, I'm sure Charlie would *love* the help," Hal said with a chuckle.

"Besides, that'll give me a chance to get to know your boy a little better," he added. "I can have some sessions with him ... start instilling a little confidence."

Although Hal kept a watchful eye on the books, he seldom ventured into The Studio. However, once Bernie started working there, Hal drove the distance at least once a week. And their sessions were helping. After only a few months, classmates who never noticed Bernie before were calling his name in the hallways.

Once high school was behind him, Bernie began studying at a nearby university. He still worked part-time at The Studio, and his weekly sessions with Hal continued. One afternoon, in the middle of Bernie's freshman year of college, Hal was at the studio going over photographs of football players.

"Hey, Bernie ... these pictures are terrific," he said enthusiastically. "You take these?"

"Yep, sure did."

"Great shots," Hal said. "Very professional. Hey, didn't you tell me your college would be selecting a newspaper editor soon?"

"Yes. In fact names are being submitted this week. Whoever gets the most votes becomes editor. Why?"

"Oh ... I don't know. It just crossed my mind that a guy who could take such terrific pictures might make a pretty good editor. You're doing so well now, but an extra boost of confidence couldn't hurt."

"What?" Bernie said. "Editor of a college newspaper? Me?"

"Sure ... why the hell not? Look at these," he said, placing the photos in front of Bernie. "I know being an editor isn't the same as handling a camera, but you're talented. It wouldn't surprise me if you ended up being the best editor that college ever had." He grinned. "You'd be crazy not to try."

"Gee, I never thought about it before. No, that's silly. No one would vote for me."

"You don't think so? Look how far you've come. You didn't have any friends when you started college. But now you know lots of people. Right?"

"Well, yeah ... I guess so. But—"

Bernie went quiet. Then he said, "I'll think about it."

"Good. That's my boy," Hal said, chuckling. "Do me a favor ... tell me when they vote you in, okay?"

That evening, when Bernie told his mother about Hal's suggestion, she was elated. "See," she said, "I told you Hal was wonderful."

Bernie smiled. "You're right," he said. "First thing tomorrow morning I'm adding my name to that list."

When Bernie arrived on campus, he walked up to the bulletin board. Quickly he wrote "Bernie Silver" under the last name submitted. On the way to his next class, he saw Dan. As captain of the football team, Dan had lots of friends, but he had only recently noticed Bernie.

"Hi there," Dan called out. "How ya doin'?"

"Fantastic!" Bernie said. "And ya know why?" He grinned. "I'll tell ya why. I'm running for editor of our newspaper. How ya like them apples?"

"Hey, Bernie, that's great," Dan said, patting him on the back. "You've got my vote. You're a lot funnier than those other guys."

"Not funnier looking though, right?" Bernie said, batting his eyelashes and flashing a Cary Grant "dashing good looks" smile.

Weeks passed.

When the time arrived to reveal the winners, a number of students were grouped around the bulletin board.

At first, Bernie acted like the outcome did not concern him. But as he gazed at the winner's box, his jaw fell wide open.

Shouts of congratulations went out for Bernie.

"Aw shucks, it weren't nothin," Bernie said, taking a little bow.

Hal was due to arrive at The Studio at five-thirty. At a quarter after, Bernie told Charlie he was taking his dinner break. He took his bologna sandwich upstairs and ate it at the reception desk. Around a quarter to six, a buzzer sounded, indicating that someone had entered the front door.

"I did it. I did it," Bernie cried, rushing to Hal's side.

"You did what?" Hal asked, thumbing through a stack of mail on the reception desk.

"I did it," Bernie repeated. "I'm the editor. You told me I should put my name on the list. Well, guess what? My friends voted for me! I'm gonna be a college newspaper editor," he said puffing out his chest.

Hal gave him a quizzical look, as if he hadn't the faintest idea what Bernie was saying.

"You remember. You told me to submit my name. Well, I listened to you. I did it right away." A smile filled Bernie's face. "I didn't mention it before because I wanted to surprise you. But today the results came out. And guess whose name was right, smack dab on top? That's right," he said, batting his Valentino eyes, "yours truly, Bernie Silver."

"Ohhh ...! So, that's what you're babbling about," Hal said, glibly. Then he went back to sorting through the envelopes. "Listen Bernie," he said. "I'm kinda busy now."

Ignoring Hal's indifference, Bernie went on, his eyes sparkling. "No, really. I made it," he said. "The students voted me in. I'm not kidding!" His enthusiasm increased. "I know ... I know, it's hard to believe ... but it's true," he said, grinning.

Hal stared directly into the eyes of the boy he had been coaching for over a year. "Listen, Bernie," he said in a manner usually reserved for a small child, "I've got more important things on my mind now."

"I thought you'd be happy for me," Bernie said, puzzled. "Aren't you proud of what I did? I thought—"

"You thought? You thought! How many times do I have to tell you? You don't NEED to think. Damn it. Just do as I say!"

Bernie looked confused. "But I did ... I did what you told me."

"Listen, Bernie, I've got news for you," he said smirking. "You're not all that special." As he said it, Hal examined Bernie's scrawny body.

It was then that Hal started to laugh.

Bernie fought back tears.

"What did you expect me to do about this?" Hal said, leering at him. "So now you're a newspaper editor. Big deal."

"B-but ... I-I won," Bernie said. "My classmates voted for me. I thought you'd be happy."

"Well, Bernie ... ya know ... if it weren't for *me* . . . no one would even know your name, let alone vote for you. Nobody cares about you. You know that, dontcha? Look at you. Bernie, you're ugly." He took in a breath and slowly let it out. "So, tell me. Enlighten me, please. Exactly what was it that *you* did? Tell me!" he shouted.

"W-well, I—"

"Damn it, Bernie ... you didn't do a damn thing!"

It was then that Bernie started to shake.

However, Hal hadn't finished his assault.

"You disgust me!" he said, sounding like a drill sergeant reprimanding a boot camp recruit. "You think you're so special," he said, his voice getting louder. "Well, guess what? You're not! You're nothing. A mistake. A zero. That's what you are ... a zero ... all you'll ever be."

Bernie cried.

"Oh, now, that's great! Are you gonna cry? You big baby! Is this who your college thinks should be their newspaper editor?"

Bernie stood still, unable to talk.

Hal started to speak, then stopped. "Go away from me. I can't stand the sight of you." He picked up the mail from the desk. "Now if you'll excuse me," he said. "I'm done talking."

In no particular hurry, Hal walked downstairs.

Charlie was developing photographs.

"Hey, Charlie," Hal said, knocking on the darkroom door. "You gotta fire Bernie!"

As he opened the door, Charlie let out a cough. "Fire Bernie?" He cleared his throat again. "Why?"

"Too many bills," Hal said, slamming the mail down on the counter.

"But Bernie's doing a great job," Charlie said.

"Doesn't matter," Hal shot back. "Do it!"

***

The following year, Bernie ran into Larry at a restaurant near campus. Larry's parents, Frank and Gloria, were among the first of Hal's followers. Larry was born in the mansion. His family moved to The Farm with the original group. They left after a few years; then moved back several times. Their accommodations included the shed and the chicken coop. In his teenage years, Larry started working at The Studio. He often went to the jazz clubs to photograph the performers. It was a welcome change from his normal routine of sweeping the floor of The Studio, cleaning up the place, and moving backdrops for the formal pictures. During several of those years, he worked with Bernie.

When the two boys met again, Larry discovered that his old friend could barely carry on a conversation.

"I need people ... I need people," Bernie kept muttering to himself.

Larry recognized those words. Hal used them in his teachings. Larry had first-hand knowledge of the down side of Hal's counseling as well as his own problems because of it.

As Bernie left the restaurant and walked across campus, he never stopped talking to himself. On the path to his bus stop, he spotted a flyer announcing an upcoming play. He picked it up and clutched it absently. On the bus ride home, Bernie glanced at the playbill.

"Hal's like a three act play," he said to the guy sitting next to him.

"Act one is the discovery stage when Hal begins to probe. This act will take as long as it takes until he uncovers what's lacking in his victim."

The man tried to ignore his seatmate, but Bernie continued his rant.

"In Act two, Hal's eyes twinkle as he gives his victim the false belief that they are finally going to make it. In this stage, Hal dishes out a heavy dose of approval, guaranteed to provide any missing psychological shortcoming. The whole purpose of this act is to demonstrate how very generous Hal is, while, at the same time, making his victim feel like a winner. This scene can't end until his victim feels happier than he ever dreamed possible.

"'Surrender your spirit. Surrender your soul!' Hal yells as he raises the curtain on Act three. His booming voice makes the audience shiver. His own body tingles with anticipation for what he knows will come next—the systematic destruction of his victim.

"Hal doesn't care about the first two acts," he tells the guy behind him. "He's not the least bit concerned about building anyone up. It's the final act he favors—the one he lives for. Each segment is carefully crafted to put him in a prime position to watch his victim wither into nothingness."

"Enough!" Bernie shouted.

The man sitting next to him jumped. Several other passengers looked annoyed.

"It's time for some script changes," Bernie told the bus driver before getting off at his stop.

Bernie walked home.

As he entered through the front door, his mom asked how he was doing.

"Better," Bernie said. "A lot better."

He went into his bedroom. From his desk he grabbed a pair of scissors, several sheets of typing paper, and glue. From under his bed, he retrieved a stack of his father's old hunting magazines.

He perused the magazines, ignoring the pictures. It was words that he needed. After selecting the perfect ones, he began cutting at a hurried pace. Soon, dozens of words and letters, with jagged edges, sat in a pile before him. He reached for his Elmer's. Bernie hadn't used it in years. The glue was almost solid. When a tiny squirt finally plopped onto his finger, Bernie swiped the white substance under the first word. He positioned it on the paper; then waited for it to dry.

When his project was complete, Bernie scribbled Hal's address on an envelope. He folded the paper, placed it inside, and located a stamp.

Bernie headed for the front door.

He needed to mail it right away. Tomorrow would be too late.

Tomorrow he might lose his courage.

"Where you going at this hour?" his mother asked. "Have you eaten any supper?"

Bernie didn't answer. Clutching his letter, he opened the front door.

Swaggering along the sidewalk, his thoughts were fixed on only one thing ... how Hal would be shaking after opening his letter.

"Yeah, that's it," Bernie said, his hand hovering above the outgoing mail slot. "Let him tremble for a change. Let him pay for what he did."

As he released his hold on the envelope, something very foreign to Bernie occurred. He had almost forgotten how to smile. He hadn't smiled in a very long time. But there, in the cool night air, Bernie Silver did more than just smile. He burst out laughing.

Seconds later he panicked.

Frantically, he reached for his letter. It was too late.

Bernie's eyes grew wide.

His fate had been signed, sealed, and scheduled for delivery.

He trembled.

Several days later, Hal was going through his mail.

"Bills ... bills ... mail from—"

"What's this?"

Hal stared at the envelope. The handwriting was childlike. No return address was given.

Slowly, he unfolded the paper. The words were shocking.

DIE YOU BASTARD

I WILL KILL YOU

YOU DESERVE TO DIE

"Who could have sent such a thing?" Hal asked Edith. Suddenly his face turned ashen.

"No!" he said, filled with horror. "Bernie wouldn't. He couldn't. Could he?"

It would seem that Bernie's threatening letter failed to bring him any relief. It was simply a matter of time before

Bernie admitted himself into a mental hospital where he spent his remaining years. Bernie didn't live to know the fate that would eventually befall Hal.

But I did.

PART FOUR

REVISITING EREHWON

Two of Charlie's children had an opportunity to see Hal in a way that the grown-ups may have experienced him. They were no longer the helpless children who lived on The Farm. Visiting Hal as adults, they were able to understand how he managed to control so many intelligent people for so long. Two others observed their uncle as his powers began to dwindle.

Kerri and I saw Hal three years before he died. During our visit, this fact became crystal clear: Instead of being the omnipotent one he professed to be, Hal was more like the wizard from Oz. The man had no real power. It was all just smoke and mirrors.

CHAPTER 53

At age thirty-five, Hal's nephew, Greg, drove out to the country with his fiancée, Monique. Greg wanted to show her The Farm he had told her about.

At the front door of the Big House, Edith greeted them warmly. Hal was in his office (at one time our living room), reading.

Greg said hello, but Hal didn't bother to look up.

When Hal finally decided to acknowledge his nephew's existence, Greg introduced him to Monique. As they talked, the conversation led Greg to ask why Hal didn't write his memoirs.

Hal replied, "What for?"

Greg answered, "Well ... for posterity."

That was when Greg got a little dose of the crap that Hal had served our parents over the years.

"What's posterity mean?" he asked, glaring at Greg as he tried to belittle him in front of his fiancée.

The fact that Monique was a pretty French woman was not lost on Hal. Before long, his magnetism came alive.

Hal invited the couple to have lunch with him and Edith.

That was an opportunity for Greg to see how Hal operated in a group. Shamelessly, Hal turned on the charm for Monique. At the same time, he took every opportunity, here and there, to put down Greg.

When Greg tried to enter the conversation, Hal cut him off saying, "I don't understand fifty-cent words."

During Hal's non-stop discourse, Greg was astonished to realize that Hal had completely dominated the conversation. At one point he started talking about happiness, making the comment, "A man can't be happy if he doesn't make his wife happy."

Greg figured that this was another attempt at playing up to Monique. Still, he couldn't help but wonder if Hal realized the irony. His uncle had treated Edith like a non-entity for as long as Greg could remember.

Continuing to develop his thoughts on happiness, Hal tried to show a flash of culture. He quoted the last words of Voltaire's philosophical tale, *Candide*, in which he offers a formula for living in a world full of misery and misfortune by cultivating a garden.

However, Hal interpreted Voltaire's words literally, using that quote to demonstrate the wisdom of his current lifestyle, in which he did a lot of gardening, canning, drying fruit, etc.

For his doctorate, Greg had specialized in the French eighteenth century. He had spent a lot of time reading criticism of Voltaire, including *Candide,* so he knew that Hal was verbalizing superficial bullshit. Nonetheless, Greg had to acknowledge that Hal was smooth and articulate. He could easily see how some people might have been led to believe what he was saying. Greg wondered how many times his uncle had used that reference to *Candide* in lectures to his parents.

***

Matt, ten years younger than Greg, was born several years after his family was banned from the Big House. He lived on The Farm the first eight years of his life and never experienced life under his uncle's influence. For years, he heard bits and pieces of stories that occurred before he was born. After getting his driver's license, Matt couldn't resist the urge to witness Hal in action.

When he arrived at the Big House, his uncle answered the door. Hal took one look at Matt and abruptly turned around. Then, without a single word, he walked away.

In a few minutes, Edith came to the door and invited her nephew in for some rhubarb pie.

Eventually, Hal joined them.

As they chatted, Matt sat across from Hal at their kitchen table.

In the final analysis, Matt didn't remember much of the conversation. Still, he had to admit the pie was delicious.

He did remember, and will never forget, the magnetism that Hal projected. In just a few hours, Matt was able to see how unsuspecting individuals might have been drawn into his uncle's influence.

***

Two years later, Joey had his adult experience with our former pied piper. Out of curiosity, at 25 years of age, he also made a trip back to The Farm.

Edith greeted him at the front door. This time, when Hal came on the scene, he was warm and cordial.

Joey hadn't expected that. It certainly was a great contrast to the cold disregard he had received as a child.

Not long after Joey's arrival, Hal took him into the library.

This room had been off limits to the kids when he was a child.

Inside the "mystery room," it became apparent that Hal wanted to engage Joey in a private session.

As Hal droned on, Joey sensed that his uncle was making a desperate attempt to enchant him. Then, as Hal must have sensed his "magic" wasn't working, his voice got louder and his fists pounded on a little table in front of him. Finally, he flashed a broad grin, as if to say, 'I nailed it.' Then he departed, leaving his nephew alone in the room.

As far as Joey was concerned, Hal's entire speech was rather pathetic.

***

As an adult, Julie also had a run-in with Hal.

At a family gathering, oddly enough, Hal was present. During the celebration, Julie was amazed to see how attentive her uncle was toward Edith. His behavior, a vast contrast to days gone by, was barely recognizable.

Julie wondered if Hal had decided to follow his own advice, that a man can't be happy unless he makes his wife happy.

Or had he simply lost his edge? Perhaps being attentive to his wife was all the man had left.

Then again, maybe he was only trying to impress relatives he had ignored for decades.

CHAPTER 54

1978

Any reasonable, thinking person might assume that after I finally got away from The Farm, that a return trip would be completely out of the question. But that reasonable, thinking person would be wrong.

Kerri and I often discussed our desire to return someday.

One morning (when I was 35 and she 39), we were on our way. If nothing else, we were overwhelmingly curious.

It was about ten A.M. when we arrived at our destination.

Kerri didn't live far away. But as often as I visited her, I never drove beyond her home. Well, almost never.

Three years earlier, in the middle of a perfectly ordinary afternoon, I found myself venturing past the three houses on The Farm. I drove up the hill—then turned around—like the school bus had always done. While my car cruised down the hill, I asked myself something I'd often pondered, "Should I really write the story of The Farm?"

Seconds later, from (seemingly) out of nowhere, a car appeared; then passed in front of me. The personalized license plate spelled out: HAL.

In that moment, I was certain the story should be told. I knew that once I found the courage, the right words would come.

When Kerri's car slowly eased into the circular drive-way, a unique sensation washed over me. The English language doesn't have a word to communicate what I was feeling. I was giddy, scared, and excited, combined with a strange awareness of being transported into a time machine that had freeze-framed my childhood.

As Kerri drove past the School House, I tried to find the apple tree where Joey and I used to daydream. Only a stump remained. The barn was also missing. Later, we learned it had been struck by lightning. The grown-ups often said that might happen.

I guess they were right about something.

Beyond the area where we played baseball as children, Kerri and I saw the Steel House. The structure looked pretty much the same as before. The field separating the houses, however, had shrunk down considerably. Correction. It had shrunk down a *lot*. How did that happen?

While Kerri parked her car, I caught a glimpse of who I believed to be Edith.

"No," Kerri said, correcting me. "That's Darla."

Wow, I never would have recognized her. I hadn't seen Darla in over twenty years. The last time I saw her was a few months after we moved into the School House. She had knocked on our door, wanting to borrow my cheerleading skirt. Yes, the one with all the seams. Based upon what Kerri and I saw on our visit (twenty-year-old high school letter jackets hanging on the clothesline in their basement) I'll bet my skirt was there somewhere. Too bad I didn't ask. I would have enjoyed seeing it again.

Being in Darla's presence brought on a mixture of emotions. Ultimately, I was glad to see her. She may have been my nemesis at one time, but that was all in the past.

She was picking vegetables in a small garden next to where the barn once stood. Following a friendly greeting, Darla led us toward the back door of our childhood home. The screen door (always covered with filthy fingerprints), and the back porch (always a mess), hadn't changed a bit.

When we entered the kitchen, Kerri and I were in for a shock. Modernization had hit the Big House. The space that held the broiler oven, where we toasted an entire loaf of bread in two minutes flat, now held a microwave. And although I didn't notice it, I'll bet there was a toaster on the counter somewhere. Naturally, the kitchen seemed a great deal smaller than what we remembered.

As the tour continued, we walked through the dining room. Memories of washing the green linoleum floor came flooding back. Instead of the beat-up couch under the window, a long table sat in the middle of the room. That was where we saw Edith. Although older and a bit shorter, she looked pretty much the same.

After exchanging pleasantries, Edith guided us toward the living room. That room was a miniature version of what we remembered. Other than that, nothing had changed in twenty-two years. All the furniture was the same, only reupholstered. The lamp, with its shade covered in photographs taken at the Sugar Shanty, was still on the end table near the couch. We enjoyed seeing that again.

Next, Darla led us upstairs.

We were curious to see the Girls' Room, but couldn't. Bernie's mother, Barbara, was napping there. With all the pain and suffering Hal had caused her son, I found it interesting that the Big House had become her permanent residence.

Compared to the picture in my memory, the adjoining hall was the size of a postage stamp. I couldn't stop marveling about how much smaller everything seemed. This was where I yelled for help when Todd's knee was bleeding. Long ago, we played elevator here, pulling two doors together to form a V. It was where we played jacks, Monopoly, Clue, card games, and learned to dance.

To the left was Hal's room, where he stayed in bed nearly all day. It was where I talked to him when I got my period, where I told him about Clyde, and where he molested me. Needless to say, I had no desire to go inside that room.

Next, we walked into Mom and Dad's old room. Nothing about it was the same. It felt odd that now Darla and her husband slept there.

Afterwards, we headed for the basement. My eyes darted toward the built-in cabinet under the stairway. I wondered if any *Honey Bunch* or *Nancy Drew* books might be there, but didn't get a chance to check.

The next room was where coloring had been done. Not in coloring books, but for the photography studio. Mom brought home the black and white wedding pictures and transformed them into beautiful color portraits. Painting the background was the first step. That's what some of the older kids did. Either because I was too young, or didn't do a good job, I was exempt from that chore. Gina and Kerri colored for hours. Homework had to wait.

In that room was where the grown-ups canned fruits and vegetables. Edith also cooked food for the dogs there. Oh, the smell! I can't describe it and pray I never have to experience it again.

As Mom colored, sometimes she helped me with multiplication tables and spelling words. This was also where I drank the liquid used in the canning process and had to get my stomach pumped.

Later, we walked outside and entered the chicken coop. Parts of the building were falling down. But we were able to walk through the room where Joey and I had taped up pictures of movie stars from the 1950's.

On the day Kerri and I returned, those walls were covered with other famous celebrities. There were candid shots of Mom with Billie Holiday and Johnnie Ray. Photos of Louis Armstrong, taken at The Studio, were also displayed. It was hard to believe that such amazing memorabilia was being held up with scotch tape, and even more shocking that they were in the chicken coop. To say that the building wasn't climate controlled would be putting it mildly.

Then we saw Hal.

As we stepped outside, he was walking toward us.

That once all-powerful one had been reduced to a tiny gnome in farmer pants, and looking oh-so-harmless. Whatever power the man once had over others was long gone. Who could have guessed the secrets he held, the lives he messed up, or the psychiatrists' children he financed through college—what with a good number of us (in later years) needing professional "couch time" to get over, understand, and rise above all the crap he had dished out during our childhood.

In many ways, I wish that Kerri and I had confronted that old man for the harm he had inflicted upon all of us, including our parents. Instead, we sat at their dining room table drinking nasty-tasting coffee (Hal's own special brew) made from chicory. Or was it soybeans? We politely sipped it, while he showed us stereo slides from days gone by.

Before presenting a slide of our mother, he paused for a moment.

"Is this one okay?" he asked, as if we might not want to see it.

We should have said, 'Certainly! That's our mother. We love her and hate the way you treated her.'

But we didn't.

"Of course," we said instead.

Before our visit ended, Hal told us, "This was once your home. It will always be your home."

What? Did we just hear him correctly? Was that supposed to be a joke? I mean ... it was one thing to go back to The Farm for a curiosity visit, but living there again?

Forget it!

PART FIVE

GETTING THE NEWS

Hearing that my mother was in critical condition was horrifying.

Learning about Hal's demise was considerably less stressful.

CHAPTER 55

1976

The night air was chilly. My two daughters, ages four and six, clung to my side, sleepy-eyed and barely awake. The three of us were standing at the top of a portable stairway, set up to greet our midnight flight from Honolulu. We were returning to California from, what some might consider, a foolish six-month adventure.

Jeff greeted us at the gate.

It was good to see him. I met him while working my former job at the airport. We dated steadily, but after two years, I grew weary of waiting for a commitment. I decided that things needed to change. Within two weeks, I had sold everything I owned, including my beat up Olds Cutlass, to begin a new life in Hawaii.

While we were apart, Jeff stayed in touch through letters and frequent visits to the islands.

After going through baggage claim, we drove directly to his apartment. With amazing panoramic views, and a fireplace to warm us on cool nights, Jeff had an absolutely awesome "bachelor pad." And with his blond hair, blue eyes, and "California kid" good looks, the place seemed made for him.

Before going to sleep, I composed a lengthy "to-do" list, aimed at recapturing my life prior to Hawaii. I planned to get up early, visit old friends, and then get my former job back. That was the plan. But after the telephone rang at five o'clock the next morning, nothing on that list mattered.

"It's your father on the phone," Jeff said, sounding concerned.

Half asleep, I stumbled to the telephone.

Why was my father calling? In the thirteen years since I lived away from home, this was my first phone call from him. Mom was always the one to keep in touch. During our last conversation, she mentioned the pain in her back and other minor health issues. But she was on the mend, or so I'd thought.

"Nita, Mom's in the hospital," Dad blurted out, his voice shaking. "She went in to have her gallbladder removed, but when they opened her up, t-they discovered she had cancer. They t-tried to get it all, but they couldn't stop the bleeding. They, uh, had to leave gauze inside. They'll n-n-need to go back in again later ... to take it out," he said.

Dad's voice sounded like it was coming from a far-off planet, and in slow motion. I couldn't believe what I was hearing.

"What? No! Oh, no!" I said.

As I listened to my father's trembling voice, my boyfriend had one foot out of the door. He needed to be at the airport in twenty minutes. He waited long enough for me to hang up the phone and briefly relay the news.

Promising to call later, Jeff jumped into his car and sped away.

I was in a state of shock, shaking and staring at the telephone. I couldn't believe that Jeff had left me. Was his job more important to him?

I couldn't think about that now. Picking up the phone, I called my sisters. I talked with one, then the other, until I calmed down.

The phone rang again.

It was Jeff. He had booked me on the next flight to Cleveland. I guess he understood more than I realized.

I arranged to have my daughters stay with friends until I returned.

A few hours later, I was boarding a plane for Cleveland. My mind went spinning out of control. My mother was dying. *She's dying.* I didn't believe it. It couldn't be true.

I fastened my seat belt and stared out of the window. The baggage crew was loading up the cargo pit. I pulled down the tiny window shade. The last thing I needed was reality. All I wanted was to escape into that safe place between somewhere and nowhere at 30,000 feet. Closing my eyes, I waited for take-off.

When the captain's voice announced the arrival of my flight at Cleveland Hopkins Airport, I was jolted back into reality. Waiting to deplane, I couldn't help but wonder how many fellow passengers were facing a difficult situation. How many others were being thrown, unprepared, into a nightmare?

Dad met me at the gate. I hugged him tight. Soon we were driving to the hospital, talking non-stop. There was so much I didn't know about Mom's condition. However, nothing could have prepared me for what I saw in the recovery room.

Tubes were hanging from everywhere.

Mom looked happy to see me, but communication (because of the tube going down her throat) was limited to paper and pen.

"Why did you leave Hawaii?" she wrote.

Forming a weak smile, I told my mother the simple truth: "The money ran out."

Mom's expression let me know she understood, but I could tell that the news made her sad. She knew how much I loved the islands.

Staring into my mother's eyes, I realized she might not be coming home. This could be my last chance to tell her what was on my heart. Even though Mom and I had many conversations regarding life on The Farm, there were important words still left unsaid. I couldn't waste another second.

"Mom, I forgive you," I blurted out. "I forgive you for everything," I said, tears streaming down my face.

The warmth I saw in my mother's eyes covered over a lifetime of hurts and filled the deepest part of my being.

"Do you forgive *me*?" I asked.

My question seemed to surprise her. But I was seeking forgiveness for lies I had told.

Her eyes let me know there was nothing to forgive.

The next day Mom was transported to a different hospital. This facility, we were told, would provide a higher skilled medical staff. Their efforts, however, only prolonged the inevitable. Soon Mom's kidneys failed.

On top of everything else, she had to be hooked up to a dialysis machine.

At that point, my brother flew into town. It was the first time all of us were together in over eight years. Mom dearly loved her only son. She was so happy he was there. You could see it in her eyes.

After her second surgery, to remove the gauze and attempt to stop the bleeding, the doctors took out the tube from Mom's nose and throat.

"They bungled it!" she blurted out.

Within minutes, the tubes were reinserted and never removed again.

We could tell that Mom wanted to say more. But those words, "They bungled it" were the last words she ever said. Although we offered pen and paper, her brain could no longer function that way. All she could manage was unintelligible lines and angles, while looking at us with tears in her eyes.

For another four weeks, Mom was in the hospital.

After the first week, I returned to California to bring my daughters to Ohio.

Mom spent the final week of her life in a coma.

Late afternoon, on the fifth day of October, Kerri, Gina, Dad and I were called into Mom's hospital room. In her final moments, she appeared to resume consciousness. She opened her eyes and lifted her head. Glancing around, Mom seemed to notice us standing beside her bed. Tears formed in the corner of her eyes.

I started praying aloud... crying and praying through tears ... reciting any prayers I ever knew, unwilling to believe the end was here.

Within seconds, my mother was gone.

Later that evening, Dad, Kerri, Gina and I walked through the revolving hospital door for the last time. We were greeted with a crisp, autumn breeze. Gazing up at the stars in that glorious night sky, I could feel Mom's presence everywhere.

"This was Mom's favorite time of year," Gina said.

Dad pulled us into a warm group hug. "Yes, it was," he said. "I'm sure gonna miss her! And I sure love you guys. I love you so much!"

CHAPTER 56

1981

How many times had the kids on The Farm tried to mimic the dead man's float in The Creek? We loved pushing our arms forward, relaxing our bodies, and bobbing on top of the water. Who could have guessed that the day would come when Hal would be doing that for real?

A local newspaper told the story.

Kerri called me with the news.

I expected to feel something. Shock. Perhaps even a bit of glee. Relief even. But what did I think? How did I feel? The truth is ... practically nothing.

It was March when Hal's body was discovered in a small creek. He had been fishing.

Had he simply made a mistake—stood up in the boat and lost his balance? As intelligent as the man professed to be, he had never bothered to learn how to swim.

Regarding his death, this comment was made: "Hal planned his life, and he planned his death."

I interpreted that to implicate suicide.

Had he been diagnosed with a devastating illness? Did he know that his days were numbered? He was 80 years old, so anything could have been a health issue. Perhaps hearing bad news prompted him to take the easy way out. Maybe this was his final "because Hal said so."

Sometimes when I close my eyes, I see him—the man who once held a small universe in the palm of his hand—ending up frozen stiff and completely alone.

I can't help but wonder ... how many secrets died with Hal that day?

PART SIX

FALLING OFF THE TABLE

My favorite picture from my childhood is near the beginning of this book. The posed photograph (a Tobacco Road photo op, if ever there was one) is of me and fifteen other kids who grew up on The Farm. We're sitting on a long, weatherworn picnic table. Today, I'd love to reunite with every one of those kids. However, that isn't possible. Three have fallen off that table.

CHAPTER 57

THIRD TO FALL

Hal's son Carter was the third child from the Erehwon Family Tree to pass from this life to the next. I don't know much regarding his passing, and even less concerning the life he led after my family moved out of the Big House. I only know that he died of cancer on, or very near, Christmas Day, 2010.

SECOND TO FALL

I can't even imagine how devastating the passing of a loved one, after a lingering illness, would be. That's what happened to Hal's youngest daughter, Darla. She suffered for a long time with leukemia.

From everything I've heard, she was very brave and fought a difficult battle with that unrelenting disease. In her final days, she lived with her sister, Elizabeth.

Upon learning of Darla's passing, sadness filled my heart. As a child, I was jealous of her. However, as I write this, tears make it difficult to type.

I now realize the truth. We were just kids.

FIRST TO FALL

In March of 2005, one of my siblings fell off that table.

Easter came early that year. The following morning, when the unthinkable news arrived, I was sipping coffee and enjoying an absolutely amazing Arizona sunrise. Brilliant pink streaks, in various shades, covered the entire sky. I was writing positive affirmations, those statements we think and/or write, about the direction we want our lives to take. I had just moved my recliner to a better viewing area.

My pen was poised in mid-affirmation when my cell phone rang. It startled me. Who would be calling so early? In an instant, my world changed.

Kerri's voice quivered.

My heart sank. "What's wrong?" I asked instinctively. Then she told me.

"No! No, you didn't just say that!" I yelled.

I ran in circles—from living room, to kitchen, then back again—all the while screaming like a maniac.

No words ... only screaming.

Kerri's response was to scream with me.

We kept it up. Couldn't stop. Couldn't speak.

Finally, Kerri was able to relay the details.

After arriving home from an Easter family gathering, Todd had grabbed a bowl of cereal and a book to read. His wife often stayed up late working on craft projects. That night was no exception.

Several hours later, she passed their bedroom door. The light was still on. When she went to turn it off, she discovered that the man she loved so dearly was gone.

I couldn't believe the news. It couldn't be true. Todd was so full of life. His presence filled the room.

Sudden death. Hearing about it changes your life in a heartbeat. It shakes you to the core. Nothing can prepare you for it. You can't quite believe it. You never get over it. One minute they're the life of a party and then ... all too soon ... their voice is silenced.

As I closed my cell phone, it rang again.

Gina was calling.

We talked and cried together, only as sisters can. Due to our unusual upbringing and six-year age difference, I didn't really know my oldest sister while growing up.

However, over time, we made up for the years when everything was out of our control.

One thing we had in common was our love of running. We ran several races together and competed in more than one marathon. There's something unique about sharing a race. Knowing the effort put forth, experiencing feelings only those who trained with you can truly understand. Only they know what motivates you to propel yourself beyond previous limits, pressing forward to the end—no matter what. They understand the challenges that come along the way and the surge of joy with the first glimpse of the finish line.

Today, I feel that special connection with all the children from The Farm ... every single one of them. Only they can fully understand what we experienced. They were at one time, and will always be ... the heroes of Erehwon.

We shared that race together.

EPILOGUE

So, what's the takeaway from this journey?
I hope it's not just that my childhood was difficult or unusual. Lots of people had difficult and unusual childhoods. Many were, I'm sure, much more traumatic than mine.

My prayer is that by exposing my deepest and darkest secret (growing up in a cult) that others will realize the pitfalls of such a lifestyle—especially when children are involved.

I once believed that if I were sitting in a football stadium, filled to capacity, and someone came over the loud speaker saying, "All those who grew up in a cult, please stand up" that I would be standing alone. Sadly, it is now my understanding that I might have lots of company. I feel certain that people of all ages, if they were willing to be honest, would begin to slowly rise up from their seats. And then, to the surprise of even their very best friends, they would be counted alongside me.

Cults are nothing new. They have been around since the 1800's. Some may be forming while these words are being written; others possibly while you are reading them. From what I understand, college students and the elderly are the most vulnerable.

People join cults voluntarily. They are happy to do so. But mind control is cumulative. I truly don't think any of Hal's followers meant any harm. I believe that with the passing of time, unacceptable behavior became acceptable. Abnormal thinking began to seem normal. And yes, I believe Hal's followers were brainwashed.

From Singer's *Cults in Our Midst* (61):

"Brainwashing is not experienced as a fever or a pain might be; it is an invisible social adaptation. When you are the subject of it, you are not aware of the intent of the influence processes that are going on, and especially, you are not aware of the changes taking place within you."

FINAL THOUGHTS

I may never completely understand everything that took place during the first twelve years of my life. Maybe it's better that way.

Perhaps revisiting my past was simply a way of realizing that regardless of anything I did or did not experience, I am a child of God. That alone makes me good enough.

While writing *Nowhere Girl*, I learned to love the little girl that I was long ago. And in the process, rather unexpectedly, I fell in love with my "self" –the unique person that I am and everything that makes me different.

I have also grown to realize:

No one had a perfect childhood.

Everyone has a story.

And, doggone it anyway, there's no such thing as normal.

WHERE ARE THEY NOW?

From Singer's *Cults in Our Midst* (262):

Although they face enormous tasks, and sometimes face them alone, children coming out of cults do survive, become healthy and happy, and lead productive lives, proving once again the resilience of the young."

NICK AND ELLIE'S FAMILY

GINA   Divorced once. Remarried (40 years), with two children, five grandchildren, and three great-grandchildren. She worked many years as a secretary. In retirement, Gina enjoyed running with her husband. They entered many races, including marathons in San Diego, New York City, Washington,

D.C., Redding, California, and even the most elite race of all: The Boston Marathon. Gina and her husband became terrific ballroom dancers. However, they do more of the "shag" now, since that's the dance of the southern area where they live.

KERRI

Twice divorced. Kerri has two children and four grandchildren. She owned and operated a successful business for over thirty years. Now retired, Kerri enjoys gardening and painting.

TODD

Married for 36 years; two children and three grandchildren. Todd worked many different jobs and owned several businesses. He passed away in his sleep in 2005. Todd was 63 years old.

NITA

Twice divorced. Nita has three children. She worked a multitude of jobs including secretary, project manager, and salesperson. After turning 40, Nita took up running. She entered many races, including the 2004 Chicago Marathon. In 2003, she crossed the finish line of the Honolulu Marathon on her 60th birthday. While writing about her childhood experiences, Nita realized the importance of supporting children through the trials of youth. For two months, she was a proud foster mother to an amazing premature baby girl. She also enjoyed being a mentor for a wonderful girl from ages 7 to 14.

CHARLIE AND SONYA'S FAMILY

A few months after Nick and Ellie's family left The Farm, Charlie and Sonya also moved their family away. Their new homes were less than two miles apart.

DENNIS

Dennis has been married for 55 years to the same woman. They have two children and three grandchildren. He's a retired college professor. Throughout his career, Dennis taught chemistry and did chemical research. He holds 35

U.S. patents, 25 peer-reviewed chemical publications, and has published four books. He was awarded a Visiting Professorship Fulbright Grant by the U.S. State Department and taught chemistry for a year in the tropics of Sri Lanka, off the tip of India.

JULIE Married, with three children, and four grandchildren. For many years, Julie worked in real estate development and management with her husband. Now, she enjoys volunteer work.

GREG Divorced. Remarried (35 years), with three children and five grandchildren. Greg taught French in college for forty years, published a couple dozen articles and seven books on French literature, culture, and film. He received an endowed chair in French at a top-ten liberal arts college. In retirement, Greg is a trustee for the American Association of Teachers of French educational endowment, a state administer of scholarships for study in France, and a custody advocate for a local children's rights organization.

JOEY

Joey was drafted by the Cleveland Indians in 1966 and played in their minor league system until 1970. He enjoyed the single life until 2009. Now he is married and retired from an excellent factory position. After retirement, he became a teacher. He has one stepson.

MATT

Married for 33 years, he has two children. Matt played four years of varsity tennis and became a full-time tennis pro after college. Currently, he has a successful career in real estate development and oversees the development of numerous shopping centers, office and industrial buildings, as well as apartments and single-family homes.

HAL AND EDITH'S FAMILY

Over the years, it seemed to unfold that Hal's children also suffered ... just in different ways.

ELIZABETH   Twice divorced. She has four children and five grandchildren. Elizabeth owned and operated her own business. Now she is retired.

CARTER   Divorced. He had three children and five grandchildren. In 2010, Carter died from cancer at, or near, 70 years old.

DARLA   Divorced. Remarried with two children and four grandchildren. Darla was a highly sought-after tailor. She died of Leukemia at, or near, 61 years old.

CHILDREN FOR A SEASON

ROSA   Divorced with one son and three grandchildren. Rosa worked numerous jobs including hotel concierge. She is now retired.

BETH	Was married and had children. Beth was fatally injured (hit by a car) while bike riding as a young adult.
LARRY	Married, father of four. He has nine grandchildren.
CLYDE	Marriage and children are unknown. Clyde died from a heart attack in 2005.
BERNIE	Unmarried. Bernie spent his final years in a mental hospital, where (as a young adult) he died from a heart attack.

GROWN-UPS

BARBARA	Barbara never lived on The Farm as a young adult. However, her final years were spent in the Big House. She remained loyal to Hal until the day that she died.

CHARLIE   Charlie had a very bad cough for many years. As he got older, he was diagnosed with emphysema, probably caused from years of smoking and/or the chemicals used at The Studio. Charlie worked there until his emphysema became too severe. He died in 1986. He was 75 years old.

SONYA   Sonya was one of the few farmwomen who married for love. She adored Charlie and suffered greatly over his passing. Sonya died in 1988 of congestive heart failure. She was 72 years old.

EDITH   Edith never worked outside of The Farm. In 2008, she was found dead on the ground where the barn once stood. Following hip surgery, Edith was confined to a wheelchair for the last few years of her life. She was 95 when she passed.

HAL   During his lifetime, Hal worked very little in the outside world. He died in 1981 while fishing in a small creek. He was 80 years old.

DEBBIE   Debbie made the dream of living in the country come true for a bunch of city dwellers. She gave them the enjoyment of hundreds of acres of trees, wildflowers, fields of clover, woods, creeks and wide-open spaces. Then, when they needed a business to help subsidize their venture, she made that possible as well. She purchased The Studio. Debbie gave and gave, and then gave some more—selflessly and happily. It is believed that Debbie put up all the cash for both The Farm and The Studio. How they both ended up in Hal's name remains a mystery.

               Debbie was in her early thirties when she died. In 2007, an inquiry about

Debbie was made to one of the younger farmwomen. Perhaps her recollection captured Debbie's essence the best: "Debbie was a very kind and gentle soul."

NICK AND ELLIE

In the last four years of their time together, Nick and Ellie had a second chance at love. After attending couples therapy, their affection for one another transformed them into teenagers in love. They purchased a camper and planned to spend their retirement years traveling the country. Sadly, those plans were never realized.

ELLIE

Ellie underwent a great deal of psychotherapy to overcome the guilt and devastating effects from living under Hal's influence for so many years. After leaving the Big House, she desperately tried to make things up to her children; and did a really good job of it. She was a wonderful grandmother to her nine grandchildren. They became a pathway to communicate the love she always had for her children. She just wasn't free to express it when they were growing up. Ellie worked at The Studio until the day of the surgery that would ultimately take her life. She only had nineteen years of freedom away from Hal before she died in 1976. She was 61.

NICK

Nick took Ellie's death extremely hard. However, he did remarry. In retirement, he enjoyed traveling, running, and golf. During a vacation to Italy with his brothers, Nick visited the town where their parents once lived. Following the death of his second wife, Todd watched over Nick for several years. In his final three months, Nita became a live-in caregiver for her father. Nick died of congestive heart failure in early 2000, two months after his 89th birthday.

ACKNOWLEDGEMENTS

To my two wonderful daughters, Misti and Christina, thank you so much for your help with those early drafts, constant encouragement and invaluable support. Thanks also to my very special son, Scotty, for helping in extra special ways.

And to all of my brothers and sisters, both literally and figuratively, thank you so much for sharing your stories. You helped as no one else could ... because you were there.

My brother left us without knowing I had plans to write about life on The Farm. While visiting him two months prior to his passing, I shared a magazine article I'd written on running. As I stood at his doorway, his last words to me were, "Keep 'em coming, Nita. Keep 'em coming." I hope this book made you proud.

To my friend, Val: Thank you for opening your home to me during my final years of writing *Nowhere Girl*. And to my friend, Paula, who stuck by my side throughout countless moves, always offering an ear to listen, a shoulder to cry on, and a place to stay. Through it all, you listened and never judged. Bless you. And a special thank you to Lenny. You touched so many lives in ways too numerous to mention. Thank you for your loving support, kindness, generosity, and beautiful spirit.

Also, a big hug to my friend, Pam Walsh Long who offered endless support and loved every one my drafts. I'm sorry to have shocked you when I revealed that my childhood years were spent in a cult. I can still see you nearly toppled over in surprise.

A debt of gratitude to my fifth grade teacher, wherever you are, for well-needed tenderness and comforting. And to the pastor of the church in Arizona: Thank you for relaying the story of Horatio Spafford who penned the beautiful hymn "It Is Well With My Soul." It was during that Sunday morning sermon, in May 2007, that I realized ... if that man could endure all those traumatic events, and still have the courage to write such beautiful words ... certainly I could find the small amount of courage needed (by comparison) to tell my story. The long and painful process of excavating memories began the very next day.

I certainly want to acknowledge my editors ... those at the beginning of the project (particularly Robert

Morgan), friends along the way (you know who you are), and especially Alicia Noack and Marilyn Janson. Thank you one and all.

A note of appreciation to a lovely lady named Rosemarie, who is as beautiful as her name implies. By allowing me to read my story aloud to her, I was able to gather immediate feedback, enabling me to further clarify a very complicated story.

Most importantly, I thank God. Without those three A.M. wake-up calls offering insight, comfort, and appropriate words, many difficult memories would not have been expressed.

And finally, a special nod of appreciation to the little girl on the cover of this book. She's been nudging me for years to get her story told. One day she whispered this ...

Although "Erehwon" does spell "nowhere" backwards, that reverse spelling can also shout "now here!" No longer a nowhere girl controlled by the past ... but now here!

RECOMMENDED READING

I found the following books helpful for understanding the nature of cults, why many people are attracted to that lifestyle, and why it's difficult to sever the ties. These books bring attention to the seductive lure that calls people into such a lifestyle, and speaks about the counseling available for those wishing to break away from them.

Captive Hearts, Captive Minds, Madeleine Landau Tobias and Janja Lalich
Cults in Our Midst, Margaret Thaler Singer
Take Back Your Life, Janja Lalich and Madeleine Tobias

The following books and tapes came to me when I needed them the most:

The Happiness Advantage, Shawn Achor
The Greatest Salesman In The World, Og Mandino
The Power of Positive Thinking, Norman Vincent Peal
The Psychology of Achievement, Brian Tracy
The Secret of the Shadow, Debbie Ford

AUTHOR BIO

Nita Clark was raised in an Ohio-based cult from birth until she was twelve years old. At first, she did not find her world strange; but over time, she came to feel overwhelmingly "different," longing for a normal life away from her unusual lifestyle.

After leaving The Farm, Nita felt that her life could begin anew; but childhood memories haunted her, sullying even her new life. Moving from Washington, DC, to Hawaii, and countless places in between, Clark never stayed in one place long. Perhaps, it is no surprise that her favorite hobby became long distance running. Since turning forty, she has participated in several prestigious races across the country.

Clark now resides in Arizona, where she has put the final touch on a profoundly healing journey. Writing her memoir, *Nowhere Girl*, ended up being the healing exercise that has helped her more than anything else.

CONTACT INFORMATION

Anita is available for speaking engagements and book signings in churches, temples, schools, bookstores, book clubs and various venues. Please visit her website at www.nitaclark.com

30548527R00242

Made in the USA
San Bernardino, CA
16 February 2016